You booked the vacation with visions of bliss.  kissed selfies, maybe even — gasp — sleep. Th you sipped something cold, and everyone would return home refreshed and glowing.

Adorable. Truly.

Because here's the truth: vacations with kids are not vacations. They're parenting in a new location, with more snacks, higher expectations, and way less patience. The car rides are cage matches. The hotel rooms are chaos factories. The pool is a war zone. And don't even get me started on "family bonding."

But here's the other truth: in between the sunscreen tears, the lost flip-flops, and the car-ride screaming, something amazing happens. The real memories. The ones that stick.

The toddler's poolside cannonball. The eight-year-old's dramatic meltdown over a waffle. The teenager's sarcastic one-liner that makes you laugh until you cry. These are the messy, ridiculous, imperfect moments that your kids will actually remember — and that you'll treasure long after the sand has been vacuumed out of your minivan.

This book isn't about doing vacations "right." It's about surviving them, laughing at them, and remembering that you're not failing. You're a mom. And that means you're already nailing it, even if everyone is crying in the hotel lobby.

So pack your bags, lower your expectations, and keep your sense of humor. Because this is *Vacations for Mommies*.

And you, dear reader, are about to realize you're doing a much better job than you think.

Chapter 1: *Just a Quick Getaway – Famous Last Words*

The Pinterest Board of Delusion

There you were, innocent, hopeful, clutching your Pinterest board and a faint belief in peace.

You typed "family vacation ideas" into Google like a damn fool.

Within seconds, you're spiralling through an avalanche of curated joy: beachside yoga in matching swimsuits, toddlers grinning near ancient ruins, families posing beside a mountaintop fire pit in color-coordinated flannel.

You are seduced.

You are weak.

You are about to spend $3,200 on flights and lose 36 hours of your life to Etsy.

It starts innocently enough:

"I just want to go somewhere chill, like the beach. Nothing too crazy."

(You are already lying to yourself.)

You open Pinterest.

Your search history betrays your descent:

> "Affordable beach house with private chef maybe?"
>
> "How to travel with kids without crying"
>
> "Cute vacation photo ideas (flattering for thighs?)"

"Cabin in woods but with Wi-Fi and minimal bears"

Soon you're deep in the false paradise of influencer mom content. You know the ones:

She's got four children, all blond and symmetrical, and somehow every photo is backlit like a Hallmark movie.

Her toddler wears a straw hat and smiles at seagulls.

Her Instagram caption reads: *"Unplugged this weekend to connect with what really matters ."*

What's not pictured:

- Her kids throwing sand in each other's eyes
- A diaper change on a public bench
- The 38 minutes of screaming it took to get that one perfect shot
- Her rage-texts to her husband while he "checked the map" and played Wordle in the car

But you, in your vulnerable state, believe.

You start saving pins to your *"Family Fun Ideas"* board like a woman possessed:

- Beach day checklist!
- DIY road trip snack bins!
- How to make matching tie-dye shirts in under 1 hour!
- 7 ways to make your toddler grateful! *(LOLOLOLOLOLOL)*

By the end of the scroll, you've lost grip on reality. You're convinced you can have:

- A budget-friendly, low-stress, culturally enriching vacation
- With your children
- Who have never sat still for more than 90 seconds

And who consider ketchup a vegetable

You don't just dream it. You begin to plan it.

You say horrifying sentences like:

"Let's do a family trip where everyone picks one activity!"

(What are you, a camp counsellor? Why do you hate yourself?)

You imagine *you* on the beach, book in hand, drink in the other, children building sandcastles peacefully like characters from a Scandinavian toy catalog.

In reality, you'll be:

>Digging sand out of your bra for three days

>Refereeing a fight about who touched whose bucket

>Holding a half-eaten string cheese and a wet sock while someone screams, "IT'S IN MY EYE!!"

And that's *before* lunch.

But in this moment, in this foolish golden hour of planning, you believe.

You believe this vacation will be *the one.*

The one where they're grateful.

The one where no one poops in a pool.

The one where you, dear mother, will rest.

You close the Pinterest tab. You open Expedia.

You whisper the words:

"Let's just do something easy this year."

Famous.

Last.

Words.

Part 2: *What You Think You're Booking vs. What You're Actually Booking*

The next phase is booking.

This is where optimism becomes delusion, and delusion becomes a $4,238 credit card charge you'll be resenting until Labor Day.

You tell yourself you're being practical.

You Google phrases like:

>"Affordable family resort with kid activities"
>
>"Vacation spots kids AND parents love"
>
>"Places where my children won't kill each other and I won't cry into room service"

Eventually, you find it.

A brightly colored website with a looping video of happy families ziplining, swimming, eating buffet waffles with actual joy. The moms are glowing, the kids are clean, and there's a line that catches your eye:

"Fun for the whole family!"

Ah, yes.
That's what you're looking for.
Something wholesome.
Something bonding.
Something with *a waterslide and a bar.*

You scroll down. There it is:

"Family Suite with Ocean View – Sleeps 6!"

Perfect.
You envision a breezy, sun-drenched room.
One bedroom for you.

One for the kids.

A balcony. A couch. A tub that doesn't whisper "mildew" when you look at it.

You click "Book Now."

Fast-forward to arrival day.

You unlock the door to your "family suite."

And that's when you realize:

"Sleeps 6" just means "has 2 beds and enough floor space for 4 people to suffer in shifts."

There's no second bedroom.

There's a *partition curtain,* a broken mini fridge, and a couch that may or may not be legally classified as furniture.

There are crumbs in the bed before you even put your luggage down.

The ocean view? If you lean out the window and risk falling, you can kind of see a sliver of blue behind a dumpster and a family of feral cats.

But it's fine. You're still optimistic. You tell yourself it's temporary. You can still salvage this.

Then you take the kids to the hotel's "activity center."

You imagined:

> Crafts
>
> Games
>
> A gentle, Disney-grade counselor named Becca who calls your child "sweetie" and plays ukulele while making friendship bracelets

What you walk into is:

> A single folding table covered in dried glue and half a crayon
>
> A teenage staffer named Brody who's texting under the table

Twelve children screaming over an UNO game with no rules

And a suspicious puddle in the corner labelled "Under Maintenance"

You ask Brody, "So what's the schedule for today?"

He blinks at you and says, "We kind of just vibe."

You leave your children there anyway because you paid $389 a night and deserve a goddamn vibe.

Next stop: the pool.

Which looked like a serene, turquoise oasis online.

But now? In real life?

It's a war zone.

Kids are cannonballing. Toddlers are naked. One child is eating a hot dog *in the water*. There's a dad asleep on a lounge chair wearing goggles. Another parent is visibly weeping into a pool noodle.

You attempt to sit on a towel and read.
You've brought a book, you fool.

It hasn't been opened. It won't be.

You are not on vacation.
You are just performing your usual unpaid labor, now in swimwear.

And yet…

There's a part of you, deep in your sunburned soul, that still believes this could be fun.
It has to be. You're here. You spent the money. You packed the snacks.
There was a whole *Pinterest board.*

Maybe it just takes a little while to settle in.

Maybe dinner will be better.

(It won't.)

Part 3: *Why Are We Even Doing This?*

But by now, you're already in too deep.

You've unpacked. You've committed.
You've paid $19 for a bucket of chicken fingers and a "house cocktail" that tastes like sunscreen and shame.

So now, as your child cries because the mac and cheese "looks weird," you ask yourself the question all mothers face in the hollow center of every vacation:

Why.

Are we even.

Doing this?

To investigate this deeply unwell behavior, we surveyed 100 moms (a.k.a. the group chat + a few women we made eye contact with in a Target Starbucks). Here's what they said:

Top 10 Reasons Moms Say They Take Family Vacations:

1. "To make memories."
    Translation: *To take one good photo that I'll cling to when I'm old and resentful.*

2. "To unplug from screens."
    Except for when the tablet is the only thing keeping someone from stabbing someone else with a pool skimmer.

3. "To reconnect as a family."
    By yelling at them in a different state.

4. **"Because it's what you're supposed to do."**
   Like flossing. Or hosting baby showers for people you secretly hate.

5. **"Because we haven't been anywhere since 2020 and I crave escape."**
   Ma'am, same.

6. **"To prove to myself that we can still have fun."**
   Spoiler: Unclear.

7. **"Because I saw someone else's photos and got jealous."**
   The honesty here is appreciated.

8. **"To watch my kids experience something new."**
   Like peeing in the ocean. Or losing a shoe on a mountain.

9. **"To get out of the damn house."**
   Respect.

10. **"Because I booked it six months ago when I was mentally stable."**
    This is the most accurate answer. She wins.

But beneath the sarcasm, there's something true, isn't there?

We *want* the good moments. We crave them.

The beach laughter. The marshmallow roasting. The accidental group hug after someone falls into a creek and everyone panics.

Even if they only last 2 minutes.

Even if they're followed by bug bites and therapy.

But still, we go.

We go with a trunk full of snacks, a heart full of delusion, and 67 chargers we will somehow still lose.

Because maybe, just maybe, this will be the year it *almost* feels worth it.

Sidebar: *Top 6 Lies We Tell Ourselves Before Vacation*

1. *"We'll pack light this time."*
   LOL. No you won't.

2. *"We'll limit screen time."*
   Until minute 17 of the road trip when you remember your children are feral.

3. *"The kids will be so tired from all the fun, they'll sleep great!"*
   Not unless they sleep *on* you, with a foot in your eye socket.

4. *"We won't overspend."*
   You will buy a $42 T-shirt with a crab on it that no one ever wears again.

5. *"It'll be good for us."*
   Define "good."

6. *"This is our year."*
   Statistically? No.

And yet we still keep going.

Which means… it's time for the most dangerous part of all.

The countdown.

Part 4: *Warning Signs You're Not Ready*

The countdown begins.

You've entered the final 72 hours before departure, also known as:

"The Hormonal Twilight Zone of Vacation Preparation."

This is the period when:

- Your to-do list multiplies like bacteria

You start ten tasks and finish none

Your partner asks, "What else do we need to do?" and you momentarily consider divorce

To help you assess your psychological readiness, we've prepared a diagnostic tool.

Are You Emotionally Prepared for This Vacation?

A Totally Scientific Quiz That Absolutely Does Not End in Screaming

Answer the following:

1. When you think about packing, you feel:

a) Calm and organized

b) Mildly overwhelmed

c) Like building a bunker and disappearing

2. Your spouse has contributed to the trip planning by:

a) Booking the flights

b) Offering "moral support"

c) Asking, "Wait, when are we leaving again?"

3. You told the kids to start packing and they:

a) Asked what to bring

b) Packed 6 toys, 1 sock, and a live beetle

c) Said, "That's your job," and walked away

4. The idea of a long car ride makes you think:

a) Family bonding time!

b) Screaming in a metal box for six hours

c) Voluntarily walking into the sea

5. Your suitcase currently looks like:

a) A neat row of ziplock bags and travel cubes

b) A rushed evacuation

c) The inside of your brain: chaotic, full of snacks, and slightly sticky

Results:

Mostly A's: Who hurt you?
You're either a unicorn or deeply repressed. You may actually enjoy this. Weird.

Mostly B's: You're a mom. This is normal. Godspeed.

Mostly C's: You are not ready. But you will go anyway. Because that's what moms do.

Real Checklist: Signs You're Not Ready to Leave Yet

You've washed the same load of laundry 3 times because you forgot to take it out
You bought new outfits "just in case" and now hate all of them
You wrote a list of "things to do before we go" but can't find it

You keep muttering "I'm forgetting something" like a haunted woman
You made color-coded folders for travel documents, but one child spilled juice on them
You can't sleep because you're mentally packing
Your partner says, "Just relax, it'll be fine" and you stare at them like they're speaking in tongues

And here's the big one:

You're already mentally planning how you'll need a *vacation from the vacation*

But hey, it's happening.

Your bags will be packed.

The kids will be semi-dressed.

And soon, you'll be in motion.

Which brings us to the final stage of pre-trip hell:

The night before you leave.

Part 5: *The Final Countdown*

It's the night before you leave.

Theoretically, this is the time to unwind, confirm the itinerary, maybe have a glass of wine and feel satisfied with all your preparation.

Instead, you're on the floor of the laundry room at 11:42 p.m., sobbing over a missing swim diaper while Googling "how to pack 7 people into a single carry-on without triggering a TSA incident."

Your partner is asleep.

Of course they are.

You are:

> Packing
>
> Repacking
>
> Yelling "WHERE IS THE GOOD SUNSCREEN?" into the void
>
> Charging 19 devices
>
> Trying to print boarding passes while the printer flashes LOW INK.

At some point, you realize someone (a child? a small, malicious elf?) has unpacked the snacks you packed and eaten 3 granola bars and a sleeve of crackers. The bag is sticky. No one knows why.

The toddler is still awake because he's "too excited." He is wearing one Croc, no pants, and demanding to bring a stuffed flamingo the size of a nightstand.

You let him. You no longer care.

Meanwhile, you open your suitcase to find your teenager has packed:

- A hoodie
- A charger
- An empty Hydro Flask
- And nothing else

You ask her where her clothes are.

She stares blankly and says, "I was gonna pack tomorrow?"

You say nothing. Just blink at her. Slowly.

You no longer use words. You vibrate rage.

At This Point, You're Sustained By:

- Goldfish crackers you found in your coat pocket
- Leftover caffeine from the cold coffee you reheated three times
- Sheer spite
- A low, primal voice inside you whispering, *"They will have fun if it kills them."*

Meanwhile, Your Partner Wanders in To Ask:

"Hey, do we have an extra phone charger?"

This man. This sweet, oblivious man who has watched you build an entire mobile logistics command center while he played Sudoku… is now asking you about chargers.

You stare at him.

You hand him the one you've been using.

You will buy a new one at the airport for $72.99. You do not care. You are choosing violence.

The Final Rituals Before Departure:

Recheck flights

Triple check everyone's IDs

Count the snacks again

Remember you never booked a dog sitter

Panic

Search "how early to get to airport with children and zero hope"

You finally crawl into bed at 1:12 a.m.

You lie awake, brain buzzing with phantom checklists and fear. You know one child will wake up at 4 a.m. with a nosebleed or some obscure rash.

You whisper to the ceiling:

"This is supposed to be fun."

The ceiling does not respond.

But somewhere, deep in your bones, you know…

Tomorrow begins the adventure.

And probably diarrhoea.

Chapter 2: *Planning – Excel Spreadsheets and Emotional Damage*

Part 1: *The Committee Meeting That Lives in Your Brain*

You wake up one morning and realize:

If we're actually doing this trip, I need to start planning.

Not "throw-a-bag-together" planning.
Not "look up the weather" planning.
We're talking cross-platform, Gantt-chart-level, Type-A-crisis-mode planning, disguised under the innocent phrase:

"I'll just throw a rough itinerary together."

Congratulations.

You've just been promoted to CEO of Family Logistics, Inc., complete with:

- Unpaid overtime
- Unreasonable clients (ages 2–14)
- One coworker (your partner) who keeps wandering off and asking, "Didn't we already go over this?"

The second you open your laptop, the committee in your brain convenes.

It's always the same voices:

Internal Mom Planning Committee:

Logistics Officer:
"Do we fly or drive? What's the cheapest day to fly? What's the least horrible layover? Do we need rental car insurance or do we gamble again?"

Nutrition Director:
"What snacks travel well? Who's gluten-free this month? Are pouches still acceptable for a five-year-old if no one's looking?"

Chief Anxiety Officer:
"What if the Airbnb has hidden cameras? What if the toddler gets hand-foot-

mouth on the plane? What if someone forgets their stuffed animal and emotionally disintegrates on I-95?"

Sanity Consultant:

"Just cancel. It's not too late. You could stay home and order takeout and pretend it's a staycation. You still have time to back out. RUN."

Guilt Department:

"This is supposed to be magical. You're the memory-maker. You can't just wing it. They'll remember this forever. You don't want their core memory to be a Wawa parking lot meltdown, do you?"

The Tabs Open on Your Laptop Right Now:

1. Google Flights
2. Expedia
3. TripAdvisor
4. An obscure blog titled "13 Must-Do Activities in [Town You've Never Heard Of]"
5. Your shared Google Calendar
6. Weather.com
7. Pinterest (a mistake)
8. Amazon (because now you need portable neck fans?)
9. A partially written Word doc titled: *"Master List (DO NOT FORGET ANYTHING THIS TIME)"*

Every tab represents a mental load only *you* are carrying.
No one else is googling, "Is this car seat FAA-approved?"
No one else is looking up the time zone difference to figure out nap schedules.
No one else is trying to predict if a historic lighthouse will "bore the kids."

Because this isn't just trip planning.

This is emotional hostage negotiation with your entire family's comfort and expectations.

Informative Interlude: Real Planning Tools That Help (But Still Don't Save You)

Here's what actual moms use to organize their chaos:

Google Sheets:
For budgeting, packing lists, and color-coded breakdowns of who is allowed to complain and when.

TripIt / Wanderlog:
Travel itinerary apps that are great until your partner says, "Wait, what time is our flight again?"

Notion or Trello:
If you're really in your Type-A zone, you'll turn this trip into a full-on project management board. (And still be the only one who uses it.)

The Notes App on your phone:
A chaotic masterpiece of reminders like "extra underwear" and "don't forget Benadryl for allergic child (which one??)"

Printed itineraries in plastic sleeves:
Used by exactly 12% of moms. Respected by all. Feared by TSA agents.

You do all this in silence.

While managing meals, fielding school emails, and keeping the household alive.

And somehow, at the end of the day, someone will say:

"So... what's the plan again?"

And you'll smile the smile of a woman who's Googled "how to fake your own disappearance" at least twice today.

Part 2: *Delegation and Other Myths*

At some point in your slow descent into planning madness, your partner will notice your growing stress. Maybe you've started muttering to yourself. Maybe your eye is twitching. Maybe you casually threatened to stab someone with a mechanical pencil.

Whatever it is, they'll say it.

The most dangerous phrase in the entire parental lexicon:

"Babe, just tell me what to do."

Let's be clear.

This is not an offer.

This is a **trap**.

Because what it *sounds* like is:

"I want to help. I value you. I'm going to be your partner."

But what it *actually means* is:

"I'm waiting for you to manage me like one of the children."

And guess what?

You're already managing actual children. You do not need a grown man with a beard and a 401k asking if 'we're bringing toothpaste.'

The Myth of Shared Mental Load

In theory, delegation should lighten the load.

In reality, **you end up doing 130% of the work just to explain how to do the original 100%.**

It's like outsourcing your anxiety to someone who's actively playing fantasy football and calling it multitasking.

You say:

"Can you just handle the hotel?"

He says:

"Sure."

Four days later, he sends you a blurry screenshot of a hotel with **no reviews, one star, and the words "convenient highway access"** like it's a prize.

The "Yeah I Got It" Lie (A Timeline)

Monday:
You say, "Can you book the rental car?"
He says, "Yeah, I got it."

Wednesday:
You remind him.
He says, "I'm gonna do it after work."

Friday:
You ask again.
He says, "Relax, I'm handling it."

Sunday at 11:37 PM:
You book it yourself because you don't want to spend 3 days in Utah on a Greyhound bus with no air-conditioning and four screaming children.

Real Tasks Moms Handle vs. What Dads Think They Handle

Actual Tasks Moms Handle	What Dads Think They Handle
Booking flights for 5 people with layovers under 3 hours	Saying "I found some flights that look decent"
Researching age-appropriate activities for 3 kids with different needs	Googling "cool stuff to do near hotel"
Building a color-coded itinerary with backup options	Saying "We don't need a schedule, let's just vibe"
Packing everyone's clothes, meds, shoes, and backup outfits	Tossing in his own swimsuit and maybe a charger
Confirming passport expiration dates	"Wait, we need passports for this?"
Budgeting meals, entrance fees, gas, parking, and emergencies	Holding a receipt and saying "Wow, that's a lot"

PRO TIP (Yes, a Real One):

If you *actually* want to delegate without losing your mind, do this:

1. Assign **one entire category** (ex: all transportation, all lodging, all meals)
2. **Write it down** like it's a job description
3. **Do not intervene unless the children are in danger or he's booking a hotel above a strip club with "continental breakfast included"**

And even then… just…breathe.
Because once he messes it up, guess what?

He'll learn.
Or he won't.
Either way, you'll still end up doing most of it.

But hey, at least he thinks he helped.

Part 3: *Everyone Has an Opinion, and They're All Wrong*

Once you're deep enough into vacation planning, you start thinking: *Maybe I don't have to do it all. Maybe I can get input. Make it a family thing. Share the joy.*

This is your first mistake.

You ask, "What does everyone want to do on this trip?"

And sweetie, you've just opened the **Suggestion Box of Doom.**

Here's what comes flying out:

The Children (a.k.a. Unreasonable Goblins)

Your 3-year-old wants to "ride a unicorn and eat only purple food."
Your 8-year-old requests "somewhere with slides, but not too many slides, but also rollercoasters."
Your 13-year-old grunts from under a hoodie and says, "I don't care," which is code for: *"I care deeply but I will resent all your choices."*

You try to show them three options.

They choose the **one that's twice your budget and already booked out for the year.**
Then immediately say, "That one's boring."

You ask them what *isn't* boring.
They say "ice cream."
They do not understand that "ice cream" is not a destination.

The In-Laws (Bless Their Hearts, But Also No)

Your mother-in-law sends you a link to a Civil War reenactment.

Your father-in-law suggests a riverboat tour "with educational value."

They both say things like:

"We did Yellowstone with four kids and no GPS in 1983. You'll be fine."

You resist the urge to respond:

"You also smoked in the car and fed us Tang for breakfast, Carol, so maybe stay in your lane."

Your Partner (Still Emotionally in 2003)

When you ask what they want to do, they say:

"I'm easy. Whatever works."

Then later, when you've planned three solid days of balanced, kid-friendly, low-drama activities, they have the audacity to say:

"Do we *have* to do all that? I kind of just wanted to chill."

Excuse me?

Sir, you had one job: contribute or shut up. You chose silence. You may not now throw vibes at my itinerary like it's a Pinterest board you weren't invited to.

Decision Fatigue: The Real Vacation Killer

You try to please everyone.

You open up another Google Sheet.

You attempt a "democratic vote" on activities.

The toddler screams.

The teen rolls her eyes.

Your partner's only feedback is:

"Can we work in some time for me to hit a brewery?"

You are now actively Googling "solo vacations for mothers who faked their own deaths."

PRO TIP: *How to Fake Democracy in Family Planning Without Spiralling*

Here's how the pros do it:

1. **Narrow the choices.** Don't say, "What do you want to do?" Say, "Pick ONE of these three things I'm willing to tolerate."

2. **Use secret veto power.** You are the mom. You are the filter. You have the right to eliminate any idea involving:
    - zip lines over shark-infested waters
    - amusement parks that cost more than your wedding
    - "rustic" cabins with shared bathrooms and no Wi-Fi

3. **Create "Illusion Days."**
   Give each person one day to "choose" the schedule (from your carefully pre-selected options). It feels empowering. They never notice the rigging.

Eventually, you'll land on a trip that satisfies… well, maybe 40% of people.

Which, in mom math, is basically a win.

And if anyone complains, you remind them:

"I'm the only one who knows where the snacks are. Speak wisely."

Chapter 2: *Planning – Excel Spreadsheets and Emotional Damage*

Part 4: *The Budget Fantasy Spiral*

Summary: "We'll keep it affordable." Famous last lie. Shows how $900 turns into $3,800 and how the line item for "mom treats herself" is mysteriously deleted.

Final line of Part 3:

"I'm the only one who knows where the snacks are. Speak wisely."

Part 4: *The Budget Fantasy Spiral*

"I think we can do this trip on a budget."

Every broke decision in history has started with those exact words.

Let's be clear: there is **no such thing** as a budget-friendly family vacation. Not unless your budget is "the GDP of Luxembourg."

Here's how it happens:

The Lie You Tell Yourself

You open a spreadsheet and whisper, *"Okay, let's keep this simple."*

- Flights: $900 (doable)
- Hotel: $600 (affordable, if you ignore the bedbugs reviews)
- Food: $300 (we'll just "eat light"!)
- Activities: $200 (plenty of free hiking, right?)

Total: $2,000.

Doable. Reasonable. We're basically financial geniuses.

The Actual Bill (Day 3 of Vacation)

Flights: $1,400 (surprise fees + "premium seats" so your family isn't scattered across the plane like lost luggage)

Hotel: $1,200 (because taxes + "mandatory resort fees" + $37/day for Wi-Fi that doesn't work)

Food: $1,100 (because "we'll pack sandwiches" lasted until hour 2 of the road trip when someone screamed "MY HAM IS TOUCHING THE CHEESE!")

Activities: $700 (because everything fun has a ticket booth, and your toddler lost his mind at the "optional" carousel ride)

Emergency purchases: $350 (forgot sunscreen, needed flip-flops, bribed children with souvenirs shaped like whales)

Coffee/alcohol for Mom: $6,472 (approx.)

Total: $11,222.

Also, your dignity. Gone.

The Disappearing Mom Budget

Have you noticed how *your* "fun money" somehow never makes it onto the spreadsheet?

Dad gets a brewery tour.

Kids get theme park hats the size of planets.

Grandpa gets a $45 T-shirt that says "Lifeguard" even though he hasn't guarded a life since 1978.

Mom? Mom gets… one iced coffee and a blister.

If you suggest splurging on a massage, the family looks at you like you're Marie Antoinette demanding cake in the middle of a famine.

PRO TIPS: Surviving the Budget Spiral Without Selling a Kidney

1. **Always double your food budget.** Kids will eat *every 45 minutes*. Even the one who "isn't hungry." Especially that one.

2. **Add an emergency line item.** For the inevitable "forgot the goggles / broke the stroller / stepped on a sea urchin" incident.

3. **Set aside cash just for you.** Call it a "self-care fund." Use it for overpriced cocktails, overpriced coffee, or overpriced silence.

4. **Never calculate the total until you're home.** Live in denial. Denial is cheaper.

A Quick Equation (Mom Math 101)

Budgeted Vacation Cost × 2.5 = Actual Vacation Cost

…and then add therapy.

You start out with noble intentions.

You end up with a credit card balance that whispers at you in the dark like a demon.

But hey, the kids will remember the dolphin show, right?
(They won't. They'll remember the gift shop keychain you refused to buy.)

Part 5: *What Real Moms Use to Stay Organized (and Still Cry Anyway)*

They'll remember the keychain. Not the dolphin show. Not the beach sunrise you nearly broke your ankle running down to photograph. The keychain.

Which is exactly why you organize. Because if chaos is inevitable, at least it should be *structured chaos*.

This is where you crack open your bag of tricks.

Some moms go digital. They've got **apps for everything** , flights, meals, bathroom breaks. Their phones look like they're running NASA, not a family trip to Myrtle Beach.

Other moms? They swear by the **notebook method**. A chunky spiral, filled with frantic handwriting and Post-its fluttering like warning flags. These are the women you'll see in the airport flipping pages like they're running military ops.

And then there's the **Notes app crowd**. God bless them. Every reminder is crammed into one unhinged scroll of text that reads like:
"PACK SOCKS - Advil?? sunscreen, dog sitter, confirm Airbnb, call dentist, buy wet wipes, DON'T FORGET"
You stop reading because your eye twitches.

And yet… no matter what you use, it never works the way you imagine.

Take, for example, the legendary **Mom Master List.**

You spend hours crafting it, categories, subcategories, backups for the backups. It's beautiful. Efficient. You almost want to frame it.

Then reality hits:

- You forget to pack the list itself.
- Someone spills juice on page two.
- Your partner says, "Do we really need all this?" and you briefly consider murder.

I once watched a mother at the gate unfold her printed itinerary, laminated like a shrine. She had *highlighted sections, color-coded tabs, even a built-in pocket for receipts.* It was glorious.

Her toddler still vomited into it before boarding.

Here's the truth:

It doesn't matter how many systems you build. Children are entropy in Crocs.

You can pack twelve carefully organized outfits in labelled Ziplocs, and your kid will still wear the same Paw Patrol shirt for five straight days. You can download three travel apps, and your spouse will still ask, "Wait, what time is our flight?" as the boarding door closes.

The point isn't perfection. The point is survival.

Because at the end of the day, whether you're armed with a bullet journal, a Trello board, or a single crumpled Post-it that says *"don't forget underwear,"* the real organizational tool is you.

The one who keeps it all spinning.
The one who remembers.
The one who doesn't get to relax.

Which is why by the time you've nearly finished planning, you feel less like a mom and more like…

…the cruise director of a ship you no longer want to be on.

Part 6: *You Are Now the Cruise Director of a Ship You No Longer Want to Be On*

You didn't mean to become the cruise director.
You didn't apply for the role.
But here you are: clipboard in one hand, snacks in the other, barking orders like a Disney employee who's worked five consecutive 18-hour shifts.

Everyone looks to you for the schedule.

Everyone asks where their shoes are.

Everyone assumes you know what's next, because you always do.

And the kicker? They call you "stressed."

Like it's a *quirk*.

Like it's not because they've outsourced every single functioning brain cell to you.

Here's what they don't see:

> You researched flights at 2 a.m. while they snored.
>
> You compared rental car policies like a Wall Street analyst on Adderall.
>
> You booked lodging that balanced price, safety, and proximity to "things to do," while also calculating the odds of someone developing food poisoning.
>
> You've memorized everyone's allergies, shoe sizes, and snack preferences.

Meanwhile, their contribution?

"I'll bring my swim trunks."

📋 The Cruise Director Job Description (Unpaid, of course)

Daily Announcements:
"Breakfast is in the cooler. Wear sunscreen. And no, we're not buying $14 bottled water when you have a refillable one."

Entertainment Coordinator:
Organizes "fun activities" that will end in tears within 37 minutes.

Conflict Mediator:
Specializes in arguments like: "He looked at me funny."

Safety Officer:
Keeps a running headcount like you're escorting a kindergarten class through Times Square.

Complaint Hotline:
Open 24/7, with zero staff, yet everyone calls.

You don't feel like you're on vacation.

You feel like you're running a floating daycare/circus with the budget of a failed carnival and the clientele of a reality show.

And somehow, at the end of every day, someone will still have the audacity to say:

"This is fun, right?"

PRO TIP: How to Survive the "Cruise Director" Trap

Build in "Mom Time." Schedule it. Guard it like the crown jewels. If it's not in the itinerary, it won't happen.

Announce Consequences. Example: "Complain again and we're doing a three-hour tour of historical lighthouses."

Delegate Like It's a Game Show. Hand someone else the map and say, "Figure it out." If they fail, let them fail. Character building.

Don't Explain Yourself. If they ask, "Why are you stressed?" resist the urge to scream. Just smile and say, "Wait until you're in charge."

Because here's the truth:

You didn't want to be the cruise director.

You wanted to be a passenger.

But passengers don't remember the one running the ship.

And maybe, just maybe, when this vacation is over, you'll finally get a break.

(Lol. You won't.)

Chapter 3: *Packing Like a Sherpa on Adderall*

Part 1: *The Myth of Packing Light*

Every year it starts the same. You tell yourself, *This time I'll keep it simple.*

You declare, "We don't need to bring the whole house. We'll pack light."

That is a lie.
That is the biggest lie you will ever tell yourself, second only to "the kids will definitely sleep on the plane."

Packing light is for college kids on a gap year. It is for single men who can live three days out of a backpack containing one T-shirt and a stick of deodorant. It is not for mothers.

You know this, deep down. Because you know your truth:

You are not packing clothes. You are packing **the entire infrastructure of a small nation.**

A Mom's Suitcase vs. A Dad's Suitcase

Mom's Bag Contains:

> Seven outfits per child (because "what if they spill" is not a question, it is a guarantee)
>
> Pyjamas for every climate on Earth
>
> A pharmacy that rivals CVS

- Snacks that won't melt, crumble, or induce diarrhoea
- Emergency rain ponchos
- Six stuffed animals
- A travel white noise machine
- Enough chargers to power NASA

Dad's Bag Contains:

- One swimsuit
- One pair of socks
- A shirt that says "Property of [College] Athletics"
- A vague confidence that "we can just buy it if we forget it"

Why Moms Can't Pack Light

Because moms don't just pack for today.
Moms pack for:

- A stomach bug that may strike on day four
- A sudden cold snap in Florida
- A "fancy dinner" that turns out to be a Pizza Hut with table service
- The meltdown that will only be solved by the exact Paw Patrol blanket your child has not looked at in two years but suddenly cannot live without

Packing is not travel prep. It is psychic work. It is betting against the universe. It is you saying: *Not today, chaos. Not today.*

PRO TIP: *How to Fake Packing Light Without Actually Packing Light*

1. **Use compression bags.** Makes you feel like you've reduced volume, even though you now have a suitcase dense enough to bend gravity.

2. **Pick neutral clothing.** Everything matches everything. Your kids will still refuse to wear it.

3. **Roll clothes, don't fold.** You will swear this saves space. It doesn't. It just makes your suitcase look more smug.

4. **Set limits.** Example: one stuffed animal per child. Then ignore this rule at the last minute because no one wants to listen to a toddler scream about leaving Mr. Floppy at home.

At some point you'll look at your three bulging suitcases and mutter, "We don't need all this."

You're right. You don't.

But you'll bring it anyway.

Because you are not just a mother on vacation.

You are a Sherpa guiding a caravan through hell.

Part 2: *You're Not Packing, You're Predicting the Future*

Packing is not about what you'll actually use. Packing is about **what could possibly go wrong.**

You aren't filling a suitcase. You're staring into the abyss and whispering, *Show me what I'll need when the toddler inevitably vomits on the rental car upholstery.*

The Mom Psychic Inventory

Band-Aids: Not because anyone will actually get cut, but because your child will remember the microscopic scratch on their pinky from three weeks ago and demand medical attention.

Extra shoes: Because one will be lost, one will get wet, and one will mysteriously smell like death.

Medication for everything: Tylenol, Dramamine, melatonin, antibiotics you're not sure are still legal.

Plastic bags: You don't know why. You just know you'll need them. For snacks, for wet swimsuits, for barf. Always barf.

The Emergency Outfit: A dress shirt for your child who swore he would never need it, right up until the restaurant host says, "Sorry, no athletic shorts allowed."

Packing = Catastrophe Forecasting

You're not choosing clothes. You're running disaster scenarios in your head like an air traffic controller on Red Bull.

"Okay, if it rains, we'll need jackets. If someone spills orange soda on the jacket, backup jackets. If the backup jackets are wet, umbrellas. If the umbrellas break in the wind, towels. If we run out of towels, trash bags. If we don't have trash bags, we die."

Every single item in the suitcase represents a future you've already fought and defeated in your mind.

Meanwhile, Your Partner's Version of Packing

He tosses in a swimsuit, a T-shirt, and says, "If I need more, I'll just buy it there."

Buy it there?

Sir, where exactly do you think we're going, Target Island?

PRO TIP: *The Psychic's Guide to Smarter Packing*

1. **Pack a medical kit.** Band-Aids, fever reducer, antihistamine, thermometer. You will be a hero when the kid spikes a fever at 2 a.m. in a hotel room.
2. **Bring one comfort item per child.** Just one. This limits the amount of stuffed-animal smuggling while still preventing nuclear meltdowns.
3. **Think layers.** Kids will insist they're cold in July and hot in December. Pack options that stack.
4. **Snacks = diplomacy.** Always keep shelf-stable, individually packed snacks handy. They solve fights faster than therapy.

At some point you'll stop and look at the mountain of "just in case" gear you've assembled. You'll think, *Surely this is enough. Surely I've covered everything.*

And then your child will walk in, look at your masterpiece of preparation, and say:

"But where's my glitter slime?"

And that's when you know.

You can never pack enough.

Part 3: *Children's Contributions, or Why You're Doomed*

You can never pack enough.
But that doesn't stop your children from insisting they want to "help."

And by help, I mean **sabotage you with the energy of gremlins.**

Scene: The Packing "Helpers"

You announce, "Okay, everyone, pack your own bag."

The toddler drags his Paw Patrol backpack into the room. He carefully loads it with:

One sock (unmatched)

Three Hot Wheels cars

A sticky lollipop wrapper

And a stick he found outside

He zips it up with pride and says, "I'm done."

The eight-year-old packs a sweatshirt, a swimsuit, seventeen Legos, and exactly zero underwear. She also tries to sneak in slime, which you will find at the bottom of her bag six months later, hardened into a fossil.

The teenager? She packs one hoodie, eyeliner, a charger, and a bad attitude. When you ask where her actual clothes are, she sighs like you've ruined her life.

Why Kids Can't Pack

Children do not understand climate. Or hygiene. Or TSA regulations.

They live in a world where the only essentials are:

Glitter

Their favorite stuffed animal (which changes daily)

And snacks, but only the wrong kind

They don't pack with foresight. They pack with vibes.

Real Talk: Why Moms End Up Packing for Everyone

Because you know the truth. If you don't intervene, your children will show up at the airport with:

One shoe

An uncharged Nintendo Switch

And tears streaming down their face because "you didn't pack my hoodie"

You will end up carrying the hoodie. You will end up carrying everyone's hoodie. You will, in fact, become a **human coat rack with snacks.**

A Conversation That Happens in Every Household

You: Did you pack underwear?
Child: Yes.
You: How many pairs?
Child: One.
You: We're going for a week.
Child: I'll just wear them inside out.
You: ...

PRO TIPS: Making Kid Packing Less of a Nightmare

1. **Lay clothes out for them.** Say, "Put these in your bag." Otherwise you'll end up with Legos and a goldfish cracker collection.

2. **Use gallon-size Ziplocs.** Put each outfit in a bag. Write the day on it. Even a 5-year-old can manage "Monday." Will they still resist? Yes. But at least you've tried.

3. **Do a bag check.** Never trust the words, "I packed already." That's a lie.

4. **Bring backups.** Always pack two more pairs of underwear than days. Kids can ruin underwear with terrifying speed.

Part 4: *The Car Trunk Tetris Tournament*

None of this is fitting in the car.
You already know it.

But you try anyway, because you're not just a mom. You are an optimist with a minivan and rage in your heart.

Scene: The Driveway Showdown

You drag the first suitcase to the trunk. It's the size of a coffin. You wedge it in sideways. It sort of fits. Victory.

Then comes the second bag. And the third. And the cooler. And the pack-and-play. And the stroller that folds "easily," except it never does, so now it's shaped like a metal spider sent from hell.

Your partner appears, coffee in hand, and says the words that could start a war:

"Are you sure you packed light?"

You stop. Slowly. Turn. Stare.

"Do you want to die here in this driveway, or on the highway?"

The Children Arrive

The eight-year-old runs out with a giant stuffed unicorn.
You say, "That's not coming."
She bursts into tears.

The teenager appears with a second duffel bag you've never seen before. It contains exactly one pair of Converse and seventeen skincare products.
You say, "That's not fitting."
She rolls her eyes so hard you hear it.

The toddler toddles over with his Paw Patrol backpack. You unzip it. Inside: one shoe, a cracker, and a Lego.
You zip it back up. You don't have the energy.

The Packing Commentary Team

As you try to wedge a cooler between two suitcases, your partner offers helpful commentary:

"Maybe if you rotated it?"
"Did you measure the trunk before packing?"
"We don't really need the beach umbrella, do we?"

You say nothing. You are vibrating with silent fury.

Finally, he grabs a bag and says, "Here, let me try."
He shoves it in. It doesn't fit. He shoves harder. It still doesn't fit. He looks at you and says, "This stuff is too big."

You take the bag back.
You re-pack the trunk in under three minutes.
It fits.
It always fits.
You are a Tetris grandmaster.

PRO TIPS: Surviving Car Tetris

Start with the big items. Suitcases first, then the soft bags.

Use every crevice. Shoes in side pockets, hats inside coolers, snacks on the floor.

Keep essentials accessible. Never bury the wipes, the iPads, or the emergency vomit bag.

Trunk rule: Once it's in, no one touches it. This is sacred geometry.

Finally, the trunk is packed.
You slam it shut with the power of Thor.

oddler claps. The teenager shrugs. Your partner says, "Wow, it's tight, but it works."

You get in the car, sweaty and shaking, and whisper, *"We haven't even left the driveway."*

Part 5: *Things You Will Always Forget, No Matter What*

You haven't even left the driveway, and already the questions start.

From the backseat:

"Mom, did you pack my water bottle?"

You did not. You packed six water bottles. Just not *that* water bottle. The emotional-support water bottle with stickers.

You sigh and say, "We'll get one later."

Congratulations. You've just committed yourself to paying **$18.99 for a plastic souvenir cup** shaped like a dolphin.

The Universal Law of Forgotten Items

It does not matter how many lists you make.
It does not matter how many times you check the trunk.
There are items you are biologically destined to forget.

> Toothbrushes. Every time. Which is why half the world's hotel gift shops look like dental clinics.

> Socks. Your kid has seven pairs at home but is now barefoot in a Chili's.

> Chargers. You packed six, but none of them fit the actual device anyone is using.

Sunscreen. You'll buy some for $22 at a gas station and discover it expired in 2019.

Medicine. The exact one you'll need at 2 a.m. will be the one you left on the counter.

Underwear. Someone is always free-balling by day three.

Scene: The First Gas Station Stop

You pull into a gas station 40 minutes from home.
Everyone tumbles out like clowns from a car.

The toddler's yelling, "I need to pee!"
The teenager's yelling, "I forgot my earbuds!"
Your partner is asking, "Did we bring the cooler?" while staring at the cooler you personally shoved into the trunk.

Inside the station, you grab:

- A pack of socks
- A generic toothbrush
- A bottle of sunscreen
- Beef jerky you didn't mean to buy
- A stuffed animal your child insists they need right now

You spend $64.77.
You hate yourself.

PRO TIPS: How to Forget Less (You'll Still Forget, But Less)

1. **Stage a "fake departure."** The night before, put everything in the car, then make the kids do a run-through. You'll immediately discover three missing items.

2. **The bathroom rule:** Before leaving, make every child walk through the bathroom and point at their toothbrush. Physically point. No pointing, no leaving.

3. **The charger pouch.** One bag, all chargers, nothing else goes in. Treat it like the Holy Grail.

4. **Accept the inevitable.** There will always be something left behind. Budget $100 for "forgotten essentials" and call it peace of mind.

Finally, you pull back onto the highway, wallets lighter, trunk heavier.

You glance at your family, all buckled in, munching snacks, already asking, "How much longer?"

And you whisper to yourself, not for the first time:

"This isn't a vacation. It's a traveling circus."

Chapter 4: *The Journey – Hell Is Other Passengers*

Part 1: *The Road Trip Hunger Games*

"This isn't a vacation. It's a traveling circus."
And the circus has just left the driveway.

The first fifteen minutes are magical. You're full of optimism. Spotify playlist queued, snacks within reach, kids buckled and relatively silent. You think, *Maybe this won't be so bad.*

Then it begins.

Scene: 47 Minutes Into the Trip

From the backseat:

"I have to pee."

From the other side of the backseat:

"I'm hungry."

From the booster seat:

"She looked at me."

From your partner, casually sipping coffee:

"How much longer?"

You've officially entered **The Road Trip Hunger Games.**

Every man, woman, and child for themselves.

The eight-year-old is gnawing through snacks at an alarming pace. The toddler is holding a banana like a grenade, one wrong move away from detonating sticky carnage across the upholstery. The teenager has vanished under a hoodie, airpods in, occasionally surfacing only to complain about the Wi-Fi hotspot.

You're gripping the wheel, counting bathroom exits like a soldier calculating enemy positions.

Bathroom Stop #1

You pull over at a rest area.

Everyone insists they don't have to go.

You march them all inside anyway.

Three minutes later, one child is crying in a stall because "the toilet is loud," another has vanished into the gift shop, and your partner is just standing there looking confused, like this is his first time seeing a bathroom.

You finally wrangle everyone back into the car.

Ten minutes later:

"I have to pee again."

The Snack Apocalypse

You carefully packed healthy road trip snacks. Apple slices. String cheese. Whole grain crackers. You envisioned handing them out calmly, like a benevolent goddess of nutrition.

Instead, chaos.

The toddler screams because the apple slice touched the cracker.

The eight-year-old demands the snack you didn't pack.

The teenager says, "This is disgusting," and texts a friend about how deprived she is.

Meanwhile, you're silently eating Goldfish you found in the glove compartment, questioning every decision you've ever made.

PRO TIPS: Road Trip Survival Basics

> Assign a Snack Czar. One kid gets to distribute food. It keeps them busy and delays mutiny.

> Bathroom = Always. If you stop, everyone goes. No exceptions.

> Entertainment Rotation. Audiobooks, movies, car games. Rotate every 30 minutes to prevent riots.
>
> Pack double the wipes. Then double again. You still won't have enough.

The car fills with the smell of crushed Goldfish, spilled juice boxes, and simmering resentment.

Someone asks, "Are we there yet?" for the seventeenth time.
You look in the rearview mirror.
You smile, tightly.

"We haven't even made it out of the state."

And so the Hunger Games continue.

Part 2: *Airport Check-In: The Circus Comes to TSA*

"We haven't even made it out of the state."
But at least in the car, the chaos is contained.
At the airport, your family is a **public spectacle.**

Scene: The TSA Line

You've barely walked in before it starts.
The toddler is clinging to your leg, the teenager is sulking, and your partner has already wandered off to "check the departures board" like it contains life-altering secrets.

You're juggling:

> A stroller that folds sometimes
>
> Two backpacks

- Three boarding passes
- Four juice boxes
- One child who is loudly announcing he has to poop

Behind you, a businessman with a briefcase sighs like he's being personally persecuted by your existence.

The Luggage Ballet

At check-in, you hoist the family's luggage onto the scale.
The agent says, "This bag is overweight."

You say, "So am I. What's your point?"

Now you're on the floor, pulling out underwear and sunscreen, shoving them into carry-ons while other passengers pretend not to judge. Your toddler grabs a pair of your underwear and waves it like a victory flag. Applause from the peanut gallery.

Shoes Off, Dignity Gone

You reach security.
The TSA agent barks:

"Shoes off. Laptops out. Liquids in a clear bag."

You have exactly 42 seconds to dismantle your life.

The toddler refuses to remove his Crocs. He lies flat on the floor like you've asked him to amputate his legs. The eight-year-old sets off the metal detector with a plastic tiara. The teenager sighs so dramatically the TSA agent actually looks concerned.

You're frantically chugging a $7 airport latte because you forgot you can't bring liquids through. It scalds your throat and tears roll down your face, but you nod at the agent like, *Yes, I'm fine. This is how I drink coffee.*

The Bag Check

Your diaper bag is pulled aside.

The TSA agent unzips it and removes:

> A suspicious applesauce pouch
>
> 14 crushed granola bars
>
> A plastic dinosaur
>
> Three unmatched socks
>
> And, for reasons unknown, a butter knife that somehow migrated from your kitchen drawer

They hold it up like they've caught you smuggling uranium.

You mumble, "It's for cutting grapes," and die inside.

PRO TIPS: TSA Survival

1. Dress like you're going to prison. Slip-on shoes, no belts, no jewellery, no dignity.

2. Pre-bag liquids. Or prepare to explain to a federal agent why you're carrying four kinds of sunscreen.

3. Kid Bribery = Essential. Lollipops, tablets, whatever works. TSA doesn't care, and neither do you.

4. Don't be nice. Move fast, look mean, channel chaos. Other travellers will fear you and clear the way.

Finally, you emerge, sweaty and broken, holding three bags, a stroller, and a half-dressed toddler who looks like he just survived the Oregon Trail.

Your partner wanders back with a Cinnabon.

"Wow, security was crazy, huh?"

You consider violence.

Part 3: *The Flight: Airborne Torture Chamber*

You consider violence.

But instead you board the plane.

It's like entering a **metal tube of judgment.**

Every passenger is watching your family shuffle down the aisle like a ragtag parade. You feel their eyes. You hear their inner monologue:

"Please don't sit near me. Please don't sit near me. Dear God, not row 17."

Spoiler: it's row 17.

Scene: Boarding Chaos

The toddler insists on carrying his own Paw Patrol backpack. He makes it exactly three rows before collapsing in the aisle like a drunk frat boy. The line backs up. A businessman coughs with rage.

The eight-year-old tries to climb over the seats like a jungle gym.
The teenager glares at you because *how dare you book coach.*

You squeeze into your row, juggling bags, snacks, and existential despair.

Your partner says, "Wow, these seats are small."
You reply, "So is your brain."

Take-off Torture

The toddler begins screaming the moment the engines roar. Full banshee mode. His ears hurt, his soul hurts, everyone's soul hurts.

You try everything:

> Bottle. Rejected.
>
> Tablet. Thrown.
>
> Lollipop. Sticky apocalypse.

The eight-year-old kicks the seat in front of her like it's a punching bag. The man in 16C turns around slowly, with the expression of someone who'd like to write a strongly worded letter to your uterus.

The teenager puts her hood up, jams her airpods in, and pretends she is an orphan.

The Beverage Cart Gauntlet

Finally, the cart rolls up. You dare to hope for wine.

The toddler grabs the ginger ale and dumps it in your lap.
The eight-year-old begs for cookies, eats one, declares she hates it, and cries.
The teenager sighs, "They don't even have oat milk," loud enough for the entire row to hear.

The flight attendant hands you a tiny cup of lukewarm Diet Coke.
You hold it with both hands like holy communion.

PRO TIPS: Surviving Airborne Torture

1. Snacks > Toys. Food distracts longer and doesn't roll under seats like Legos.

2. Suckers for take-off and landing. Helps with ear pressure, buys five minutes of peace.

3. Pack one surprise toy. Nothing fancy, just something new to buy you thirty minutes.
4. Noise-cancelling headphones. For you, not the kids. Block the chaos. Pretend you're alone.

The Shame Spiral

An hour in, the toddler finally sleeps — on your lap, pinning you in place like a sweaty, drooling paperweight. You have to pee so badly you're considering adult diapers for next trip.

The eight-year-old whispers, "I'm bored," every three minutes.
The teenager refuses to share her charger.
Your partner? Asleep. Mouth open. Snoring.

You look around at the sea of annoyed faces. You know what they're thinking.

You *are* that family.
The one everyone dreads.
The horror story they'll retell at dinner parties.

And in this moment, you don't care.

Because at least the toddler is asleep.

Part 4: *Other Passengers: The True Villains*

At least the toddler is asleep.
You dare to exhale.
And then you feel it: the heat of judgment.

Because the real villains of air travel are not your children.
They are the other passengers.

Scene: The Cast of Row 17

The Businessman in 16C

He sighs loudly every time your child moves. He types furiously on his laptop, pretending his work is so important that toddler giggles might collapse the global economy. At one point he mutters, "Unbelievable," as if you birthed these children specifically to ruin his day.

The Grandmother in 18A

She leans forward to tell you, "When mine were little, I just gave them coloring books and they were perfect angels." You nod politely while imagining pushing her tray table so hard her ginger ale baptizes her cardigan.

The Influencer in 15B

She documents every second of her trip with selfies. She posts, "Love traveling " while glaring at your child like you personally cancelled her sponsorship deal with Sephora.

The Guy Who Reclines Immediately

Seat goes back the second the seatbelt light turns off. Now your eight-year-old has six inches of space and is kicking his seat with the fury of a Spartan warrior. He turns, offended, as if this is not the natural consequence of his choices.

The Woman Who Stares

No words. Just relentless, icy glares every time your toddler squeaks. She looks at you like you brought a swarm of locusts into the cabin. You try smiling at her. She does not smile back. She will never smile again.

The Public Shaming

Your toddler shifts in his sleep and lets out a squeaky fart. Half the row snickers. The businessman groans. The teenager rolls her eyes so hard you're afraid they will get stuck.

You sink lower in your seat, clutching the safety card like it might explain how to eject yourself mid-flight.

PRO TIPS: Handling Passenger Villains

1. Noise management. Hand out lollipops or tablets without shame. You're not raising philosophers at 30,000 feet.
2. Strategic apologies. A quick "Sorry, he's tired" disarms 80 percent of glares. The other 20 percent are sociopaths. Ignore them.
3. Pre-emptive humor. If a kid shrieks, lean over and whisper, "That's his podcast voice." You'll get at least one laugh, which counts as a win.
4. Mental armor. Remember: you will never see these people again. Their judgment evaporates the second the wheels hit the ground.

You glance around your section of the plane.

It is you, your family, and a jury of strangers silently convicting you of the crime of motherhood.

You think, *Fine. I'll take the sentence.*

Because at least the toddler is still asleep.

Part 5: *Arrival: You've Made It, But at What Cost?*

Because at least the toddler is still asleep.
And then the plane lands.

There should be fanfare. Balloons. Maybe a gospel choir. Instead there is only the fluorescent hum of the airport and the collective groan of passengers standing up too early.

Arrival is supposed to feel triumphant. You survived TSA, turbulence, and public shaming. Instead, you feel like someone who just staggered out of a bunker after a minor apocalypse.

Here's the thing no one tells you about travel with children: **reaching your destination is not relief. It is merely a change of battleground.**

You are now:

> Sweaty
>
> Carrying six bags
>
> Holding one child who has gone completely limp like a corpse
>
> And trying to remember which rental car shuttle is yours while another kid is crying about her missing hoodie

You're in paradise. Technically. But it feels like you just crawled out of a war trench.

Parents always imagine that arrival will flip a switch. That the misery will vanish and vacation joy will take over. It doesn't.

Because the second you land, the questions start:

> Where's the luggage?
>
> Where's the stroller?
>
> Where's the bathroom?
>
> Where's the exit?
>
> Where's my will to live?

Everyone's cranky. Everyone's hungry. And somehow, despite packing enough snacks to feed a small village, **all food has disappeared.**

The Great Letdown

You thought stepping off the plane would feel like a release. Instead it feels like checking into a new level of purgatory.

At the hotel, you're greeted with "Check-in isn't until 3 p.m." even though it's 11:00 and your children are unravelling before your eyes. You think, *Maybe we can explore the city until then.*

You will not. You will sit in the lobby, praying for mercy, while your toddler rolls on the carpet and the teenager hisses that she "just wants privacy."

Observational Truth Bombs

> Lost luggage is a guarantee. It is never the bag you can spare. It is always the one with every pair of underwear.
>
> Children do not reset. They arrive tired, hungry, sticky, and remain tired, hungry, sticky until the trip is over.
>
> Your partner will say, "We made it!" with joy. You will want to reply, "We survived." Subtle difference.
>
> The fantasy of arrival is always better than the reality. In your head: cocktails by the pool. In reality: you're rinsing Goldfish crumbs out of a car seat.

The truth is, arrival is not a finish line. It is simply the start of the next phase of chaos.

You'll get through it. You'll unpack, you'll re-pack, you'll navigate the new battlefield of hotel rooms and sightseeing.

But right now, as you collapse on a questionable bedspread with your children bickering over who gets the "good pillow," one thought dominates your exhausted brain:

"We left home for this?"

Chapter 5: *The Lodging Situation — Where Sleep Goes to Die*

Part 1: *Check-In Desk of Broken Dreams*

"We left home for this?"
But the car is parked, the plane has landed, the kids are still alive. You cling to the one beacon of hope left: the lodging.

The glossy photos promised clean sheets, fluffy pillows, maybe even a pool with a swim-up bar. You pictured yourself sliding a keycard into a door, dropping bags, and sighing with relief like a glamorous woman in a commercial.

Instead, you are standing in a lobby that smells like chlorine, feet sticking to the tile, while your toddler licks the luggage cart.

Scene: The Hotel Lobby

You drag yourself to the check-in desk. Your hair is plastered to your forehead. Your kids are circling the lobby like caffeinated pigeons.

The desk clerk greets you with a smile so fake it should be in a wax museum.

"Your room won't be ready until three."

It is currently 11:07 a.m.

Your toddler is already screaming.

Your teenager says, "I told you we should have stayed somewhere nicer."

You smile tightly and say, "Of course. No problem."

Inside, you are screaming so loudly dogs three towns over can hear it.

The Airbnb Version

Maybe you thought you'd be clever and avoid hotels altogether. A cozy Airbnb, you said. It'll be "more space for less money," you said.

Instead, you're greeted by:

> A faint smell of mildew
>
> A futon labelled "second bedroom"
>
> And a guest binder that includes both Wi-Fi instructions and passive-aggressive notes about recycling

The kids ask if there's a pool.

You say no.

They cry.

You cry.

PRO TIPS: Surviving Check-In

1. Always ask for early check-in. They will say no. Ask anyway. Sometimes desperation works.
2. Pack a "lobby survival kit." Snacks, wipes, a tablet, and something that distracts you from the judgmental stares of other guests.

3. Never believe the photos. If it looks too good to be true, it is. That "spacious living room"? A wide-angle lens. That "king bed"? A queen with confidence issues.

4. Lobby lobbyists. One adult checks in while the other keeps kids outside. It lowers your odds of losing a deposit before you even get the key.

Finally, after thirty minutes of paperwork, signatures, and whispered threats to your offspring, you get the room key.

You hold it aloft like a golden ticket. Victory.

But the door to that room?
That is where the real horror begins.

Part 2: *One Room, Four People, Zero Boundaries*

The real horror begins when you slide the keycard, fling open the door, and discover what "family suite" really means.

It means one bed, a pull-out couch that smells faintly of feet, and a lamp that flickers like a horror movie prop.

The toddler immediately claims the king bed by launching himself face-first into the pillows.
The teenager gasps like she has just witnessed a crime.

"I am not sharing a room with them."

You reply, "Yes you are."
She replies, "Then I'll just sleep outside."
You reply, "Great. Don't forget your hoodie."

The Bed Assignments

The eight-year-old insists on the middle of the king bed. Non-negotiable.

The toddler also insists on the middle. Non-negotiable.

Your partner says, "I don't mind the pull-out couch."

You say, "Yes you do."

He says, "No, I don't."

You both know he does.

By nightfall, you are in the middle of the king bed, a toddler's foot in your throat, while your partner snores peacefully on the pull-out like he's auditioning for a mattress commercial.

The Thermostat Wars

You like the room cold.

Your partner likes it tropical.

The kids don't care, except they will wake you at 2 a.m. to announce, "It's too hot" or "It's too cold" or, "I can't sleep because the air conditioner sounds like a dragon."

You spend the night creeping over to the thermostat like a burglar, changing it one degree at a time. By morning, no one is satisfied.

The Suitcase Explosion

You tried. You really did. You thought, *We'll keep things organized.*

Within 30 minutes, the room looks like a thrift store exploded. Clothes are draped over lamps. Toothbrushes are balanced on the TV. Someone left a sock in the ice bucket.

The toddler unpacks your carefully folded outfits and hides them behind the curtains. The teenager asks, "Where's my makeup bag?" You say, "In your suitcase." She says, "No, it's not." You find it in the mini fridge next to a Capri Sun.

PRO TIPS: Surviving One-Room Chaos

1. Bring a white noise machine. Or use your phone. Drown out snoring, traffic, and the sound of your child whispering, "I'm not tired."
2. Claim a corner. Even a chair. Make it your sanctuary. Guard it like treasure.
3. Overpack pyjamas. Kids will spill juice, toothpaste, or entire bowls of mac and cheese on theirs.
4. Hide snacks. If the kids find them all at once, you will lose your only leverage.

You collapse onto the bed at midnight, body wedged between two children who smell faintly of sunscreen and despair.

Your partner sighs happily from the pull-out couch.

"Not bad, right?"

You stare into the dark.

This is not lodging.

This is survival camp.

Part 3: *The Bathroom Wars*

This is not lodging. This is survival camp. And every survival camp has a single most valuable resource.

Here, it isn't food. It isn't beds. It isn't even Wi-Fi.

It's the bathroom.

Scene: Morning in the Shared Bathroom

The bathroom door clicks shut at 7:05 a.m. The teenager has entered.

By 7:08, you already regret every choice that led to this moment. You can hear music blasting from her phone, the sound of hairspray, and the unmistakable gurgle of someone wasting precious hot water.

From the toddler:

"I need to pee."

From the eight-year-old:

"I need to brush my teeth."

From your partner, lying on the pull-out couch, scrolling on his phone:

"I'll take a shower after her."

From you, standing in the hallway with a full bladder and murder in your eyes:

"No. You won't."

The Teenager's Reign of Terror

You knock gently.

"Sweetie, can you hurry? Other people need the bathroom."

From inside:

"I just got in here!"

That is a lie. She has been in there for twenty minutes.

When she finally emerges, the counter is covered in mascara tubes, hair straighteners, and mysterious liquids that smell like chemicals and regret. There are wet towels on the floor, toothpaste sprayed on the mirror, and the toilet paper roll has vanished into the void.

She sighs and says, "It's not my fault there's no space."
You consider shaving your head and moving into a convent.

The Toddler Invasion

The toddler waddles in.

You follow, because he cannot be trusted alone.

In three minutes he has:

>Unrolled the entire toilet paper roll into the trash

>Dropped his toothbrush into the toilet

>Splashed water all over the counter while "washing hands"

>Announced loudly, "Mommy is peeing!" through the open door

Privacy is a fairy tale. Dignity is extinct.

The Eight-Year-Old's Demands

Next in line is the eight-year-old. She brushes her teeth like she is auditioning for a horror movie. Toothpaste foam everywhere. It drips down her chin. It streaks the counter. At one point, you are fairly sure she spits into the sink and misses.

She then asks, "Can I paint my nails?"
You say, "Absolutely not."
She says, "But why not?"
You say, "Because this isn't a spa."
She says, "It could be."
You close your eyes and count to ten.

Dad's Spa Retreat

Finally, it's your partner's turn.

He enters, humming.

He stays in there for twenty-eight minutes.

He showers. He shaves. He emerges in a towel, fresh and relaxed, saying things like:

"That felt good."

Meanwhile, you have not peed since yesterday.

PRO TIPS: Surviving Bathroom Chaos

1. Assign shifts. Teens first, toddlers last. You go when you can. Dad waits until checkout.
2. Bring a hanging toiletry bag. Hotels never have enough counter space. Claim vertical real estate.
3. Travel with flushable wipes. Kids will find ways to get sticky at 6 a.m. in a hotel. Wipes buy you sanity.
4. Enforce the five-minute rule. Except for Dad. He will ignore it anyway.
5. Use the lobby bathroom. It's cleaner, quieter, and no one will follow you in yelling about missing toothpaste.

By 9:15, everyone has technically "used" the bathroom. The toddler is damp, the eight-year-old smells like bubblegum toothpaste, the teenager looks like she's headed to Fashion Week, and your partner is glowing like a spa model.

You? You are still waiting your turn.

Because in the bathroom wars, the mother is always the last to fall.

Part 4: *Sleep? That's Cute*

The bathroom wars end. The pyjamas are on. The bags are piled in corners like sad luggage fortresses. You think, *Finally, maybe we can sleep.*

That is adorable. You are adorable. Sleep is not part of this trip.

Scene: Night One

9:30 p.m. The toddler is thrashing in the middle of the bed like he's auditioning for a stunt show. You whisper, "Shhh, go to sleep." He whispers back, "I can't. My toes are itchy."

9:45. The eight-year-old says, "I forgot Mr. Snuggle." You dig through four bags until you find him stuffed inside a shoe. The child sighs, content, and then immediately says, "I'm not tired."

10:15. The teenager is scrolling TikTok with her screen brightness set to "sun." You say, "Turn it off." She says, "It's not even loud." You consider confiscating the phone and hiding it in the hotel ice machine.

10:47. Your partner starts snoring. Loudly. Not cute snoring, but the freight-train-wheezing kind that rattles the lamp. You nudge him. He says, "I wasn't asleep."

Midnight Hour

12:06. The toddler wakes up crying because "the dark is scary." You flip on the bathroom light for a nightlight glow. Now the teenager groans, "It's too bright."

12:40. The eight-year-old kicks you in the kidney. You consider filing a police report.

1:23. The toddler whispers, "Mommy, I love you." Your heart melts. Then he sneezes directly in your face.

The Witching Hours

2:15. Someone flushes the toilet in the room above you. The toddler sits up and screams like the building is under attack.

3:00. Your partner rolls over, taking the blanket with him. You are left clinging to a fitted sheet like a shipwreck survivor.

4:07. The eight-year-old sleep-talks: "The unicorns are coming." You whisper back, "Tell them to bring coffee."

The Morning "Wake-Up"

5:12. The toddler pops up like a jack-in-the-box and yells, "IS IT MORNING YET?"

It is not morning. You say, "Go back to sleep." He says, "But I'm hungry."

5:30. The eight-year-old announces she's cold. You add another blanket. She immediately says she's hot.

5:45. The teenager moans, "Why are we even here?" You are tempted to say, "So I can suffer in a new location."

6:00. Your partner sits up, stretches, and says, "Wow, I actually slept great."

You stare at him, hollow-eyed, considering divorce.

💡 PRO TIPS: Surviving Hotel Room "Sleep"

1. White noise machine. Essential. Blocks out snoring, hallway noises, and mysterious thuds from upstairs.

2. Separate bedding. If possible, give kids their own blanket. Otherwise you'll be in a tug-of-war all night.

3. Strategic bed placement. Put toddlers against the wall, not the edge. Or spend the night catching them mid-fall like a goalie.

4. Sleep mask and earplugs. Not for the kids. For you. Protect your last shred of sanity.

5. Accept reality. You will not sleep. You will nap with interruptions. Set expectations low. Really low.

By 7:00 a.m., the kids are bouncing, your partner is whistling, and you are a husk of a human being.

Vacation lodging is not for rest. It is a nightly hostage situation with snacks.

Part 5: *Morning After, Regret Before*

Vacation lodging is not for rest. It is a nightly hostage situation with snacks.

And yet, somehow, morning still arrives. Not gracefully, not gently. It barges in like a SWAT team.

You are wrecked. You look like you've just crawled out of a bunker. Your partner, of course, is chipper. "I slept great," he says, stretching like a cat. You briefly imagine smothering him with a hotel pillow.

The kids are sticky. Always sticky. You do not know where the stickiness comes from. You stopped giving them juice boxes six hours ago, but somehow they are coated in sugar glue, hair matted like feral raccoons.

The Breakfast Mirage

You think, *Maybe food will help.*

You shuffle toward the "continental breakfast." Which is always a depressing buffet of mystery eggs, damp waffles, and yogurt cups that expired sometime during the Obama administration.

Your toddler eats three packs of butter straight from the container.

Your eight-year-old demands Froot Loops, fills the bowl, takes one bite, and abandons it.

The teenager mutters, "This is disgusting," while eating exactly nothing.

Your partner piles his plate with eggs and bacon like he's at a Vegas buffet and says, "This isn't so bad."

You sip bitter coffee from a Styrofoam cup and silently draft divorce papers in your head.

The Emotional Hangover

The cruel joke of vacation lodging is that you wake up more tired than you were at home. You thought you were escaping the grind. Instead you are marinating in it, just with worse pillows and strangers walking past your door at all hours.

At home, exhaustion feels routine. Here, it feels insulting. *I paid money to feel this tired?*

PRO TIPS: Morning-After Survival

1. Bring real coffee. Hotel coffee is brewed sadness. A travel French press can save your life.

2. Lower expectations. Breakfast is not nourishment, it is a holding pen until you can find real food.

3. Schedule nothing for the morning. You won't be productive. Accept it.

4. Always pack snacks. Your kids will reject hotel food and still demand calories every seven minutes.

The Regret Spiral

By 9:00 a.m., you're standing in a lobby that smells like wet carpet, staring at your family. Everyone is cranky, everyone is loud, everyone looks like they lost a bar fight.

You wonder why you didn't just stay home.

Then you pull out your phone and Google, "all-inclusive resorts with on-site childcare."

And for the first time all morning, you feel hope.

Chapter 6: *Activities — Fun or a Trap?*

Part 1: *The Planning Delusion*

And for the first time all morning, you feel hope.

Until you remember the activities.

Vacation activities are the great lie parents tell themselves. You picture smiling children, scenic views, and candid photos worthy of Christmas cards. You imagine family bonding, laughter, and phrases like, "This was the best day ever."

In reality, activities are where vacations go to die.

The Fantasy

You book an excursion: a dolphin encounter, a city tour, maybe kayaking. You think, *This will be magical.*

You picture yourself in a sundress, holding your toddler's hand as dolphins leap in the distance. The sun is shining, your children are laughing, and your partner is gazing at you with renewed desire.

The Reality

Here is what actually happens:

> Your toddler refuses to put on the life vest.
>
> Your eight-year-old asks, "Can we go back to the hotel?" every three minutes.
>
> Your teenager mutters, "This is lame," while scrolling Instagram.
>
> Your partner "accidentally" books the wrong day and you end up paying triple.

The dolphins do not leap. The dolphins look bored. One sneezes. Your toddler screams in terror.

Scene: The Morning of an Excursion

You wake up early. Everyone is cranky. You pack snacks, sunscreen, towels, and water bottles. You double-check tickets. You hustle the family into the car.

From the backseat:

"I don't want to go."

You say, "We paid $400 for this. You're going."

By the time you arrive, the toddler has spilled juice on his only clean outfit, the eight-year-old is crying because she forgot Mr. Snuggle, and the teenager refuses to get out of the car.

You smile weakly at the tour guide, who looks like he regrets his career choices.

The Emotional ROI

Parents think activities will build memories. They do, but not the kind you want.

What your children remember is:

- The time you made them walk too far in the heat.

- The time they cried in a museum gift shop.
- The time you yelled, "We're here to have fun, damn it."

Meanwhile, you remember spending $600 to hear, "This sucks."

PRO TIPS: Cutting Activity Pain in Half

1. Pick one "big" activity. Just one. Not seven. Kids will revolt by day two.
2. Schedule downtime. A pool counts as an activity. So does lying in bed with tablets.
3. Know your audience. Don't book a three-hour walking tour for kids who whine after three blocks.
4. Always overpack snacks. Hunger destroys family fun faster than sunburn.
5. Budget for bribes. Ice cream, small toys, anything to keep spirits from collapsing mid-activity.

Vacation activities are not about joy. They are about survival. They are the tax parents pay for believing in Instagram.

And still, you'll book them again next year. Because hope dies last.

Part 2: *Theme Parks: The Seventh Circle of Hell*

Hope dies last. Which is why you find yourself marching your family through the gates of a theme park, $642 poorer before you've even seen a ride.

You tell yourself this will be magical. You say words like "memories" and "happiest place on earth." But deep down, you know. This is not happiness. This is penance.

Scene: The Morning Rush

The kids are bouncing, full of excitement. The toddler is dressed like a miniature pirate. The eight-year-old has Minnie Mouse ears. The teenager looks like she's attending a funeral.

You push through crowds of strollers, backpacks, and sweaty dads. The music is cheerful, but the vibe is ominous.

Your partner says, "Let's grab a map."
You snap, "There's an app."
Your teenager says, "The Wi-Fi sucks."
The toddler announces, "I'm hungry."

It is 9:07 a.m.

The Lines

This is the true theme park experience. Lines. All day. For everything.

Lines for rides.
Lines for food.
Lines for bathrooms.
Lines for the privilege of standing in other lines.

The eight-year-old asks, "How much longer?" every ninety seconds. You say, "Almost there." You are lying.

After forty-five minutes, you reach the front. The toddler immediately screams, "I don't want to go on!" You carry him anyway, whispering, "We paid for this."

The Food

By noon, everyone is starving. You spend $74.50 on three chicken nugget meals and a churro.

The toddler eats ketchup with his fingers.

The eight-year-old declares the nuggets are "weird."

The teenager takes one bite of the churro, says, "I'm full," and throws it away.

Your partner eats everything else, then says, "This wasn't so bad."

You eat nothing. You are running on resentment.

Scene: The Parade

You think, *At least the parade will be nice.*

You stake out a spot on the curb. The toddler lies face-down on the pavement. The eight-year-old whines, "I can't see." The teenager scrolls on her phone.

The parade begins. Music, floats, dancers. It is objectively impressive.

Your toddler bursts into tears because the mascot waved "too hard."
The eight-year-old begs for cotton candy. You give in. She eats three bites and drops it. It melts into your shoe.
The teenager sighs, "This is so cringe."

You watch a man in a giant mouse costume dance by and think, *I could have been a lawyer.*

The Meltdown Hour

Around 3:00 p.m., everything collapses. The toddler refuses to walk. You carry him, sticky and limp, like a sack of melted gummy bears.

The eight-year-old cries because she wants to go on the same ride again.
The teenager demands to be left alone.
Your partner suggests, "Maybe we should split up?" which you know means he wants to disappear for beer.

You are sweating through your clothes. Your Fitbit says you've walked nine miles. You consider faking a medical emergency just to sit down.

The Gift Shop Trap

You attempt to leave. But you cannot. Because every exit runs through a gift shop.

The toddler grabs a $47 bubble wand.

The eight-year-old demands a $62 stuffed animal.

The teenager rolls her eyes and mutters, "This is all so commercial."

You say no. They scream.

You say yes. You cry.

PRO TIPS: Surviving the Seventh Circle

1. Set expectations low. Tell yourself in advance: you will stand in lines, spend too much money, and cry at least once.

2. Hydrate aggressively. Water is $6 a bottle. Bring your own or prepare to remortgage your house.

3. Use the app. It will not make lines shorter, but it gives you the illusion of control.

4. Schedule breaks. Air conditioning is not optional. Neither is caffeine.

5. Pick one splurge. Buy the overpriced souvenir up front. It shuts kids up for at least twenty minutes.

At 9:00 p.m., you drag your family back to the parking lot. The toddler is asleep in the stroller, drooling. The eight-year-old is sticky, carrying a balloon that will deflate by morning. The teenager has posted thirty-seven complaints on Instagram.

Your partner says, "That was fun."

You whisper, "Never again."

And next year, you will come back.

Because hope dies last.

Part 3: *"Fun" Educational Activities*

Hope dies last. Which is why, after the theme park, you decide to "balance things out" with something more meaningful. Something enriching. Something that will broaden your children's horizons and justify the thousands you've already haemorrhaged.

You say the cursed words:

"Let's do something educational."

Scene: The Museum

You herd your family into a museum. It could be art, history, science — it doesn't matter. The moment you enter, the kids all turn into professional critics of misery.

The toddler runs straight toward a priceless exhibit, hands outstretched like he's auditioning for *Mission: Impossible.*
The eight-year-old immediately says, "I'm bored."
The teenager says, "Can I just sit in the café?"
Your partner looks at the brochure and says, "This could be interesting," which is a phrase that should be banned from vacations.

The Toddler Experience

The toddler is not here for history or culture. He is here for buttons. If there's an interactive screen, he will bang it with the fury of Thor. If there's not, he will press imaginary buttons on the walls until security gets nervous.

Eventually, he announces, "I need to poop," at the farthest possible point from the restroom. You sprint through two exhibits on ancient pottery, clutching him like a ticking time bomb.

The Eight-Year-Old Experience

The eight-year-old does not see art. She sees opportunities to whine.

"This is boring."
"These statues are creepy."
"Why can't we go to the gift shop?"

You attempt to explain the significance of a dinosaur fossil. She yawns. She then asks, "Can we get ice cream after this?" seventeen times in under five minutes.

The Teenager Experience

The teenager walks three steps behind the family, hood up, earbuds in. She occasionally glances at an exhibit long enough to take a blurry Snapchat captioned, "Kill me."

When you ask her opinion on the art, she says, "It's fine." When you press further, she says, "Why do you care?"

At one point she vanishes entirely. You find her in the lobby, plugged into an outlet, charging her phone.

The Parent Experience

You try. You really try. You read the plaques. You nod thoughtfully. You say things like, "Fascinating," while holding a toddler who smells suspiciously like applesauce.

Your partner says, "It's good for them." You reply, "So is waterboarding."

After ninety minutes, you've seen about twelve percent of the museum. You are mentally drained, physically sticky, and financially lighter after spending $118 in the gift shop on a stuffed penguin, a pencil sharpener, and a book no one will ever read.

PRO TIPS: Surviving Educational Fun

1. Keep it short. One hour, max. Any longer and kids start plotting mutiny.
2. Bribe early. Promise ice cream if they behave. Yes, it is manipulation. It also works.
3. Interactive first. Skip the paintings. Head straight for the buttons, the fish tanks, or anything that makes noise.
4. Gift shop strategy. Give each kid a set amount of money. Once it's gone, it's gone. Otherwise you'll be guilted into buying $35 snow globes.
5. Don't over-romanticize. You are not raising philosophers. You are raising children who will someday say, "Remember that boring museum?" and laugh.

When it's finally over, you stumble into daylight.

The toddler is crying. The eight-year-old is sticky. The teenager is already posting online: *Worst day ever.*

Your partner says, "Well, at least we learned something."

You nod. You did learn something.
You learned never to do this again.

Part 4: *Outdoor Adventures, Indoor Regrets*

You learned never to do this again.

Which is why, naturally, you're packing everyone into the car for a day outdoors.

Because apparently vacations require "fresh air" and "adventure."

Scene: The Family Hike

You picture it like a commercial. Happy children skipping along trails, sunlight filtering through the trees, everyone holding reusable water bottles and laughing.

Reality arrives immediately.

The toddler refuses to walk, demanding to be carried like an entitled prince. The eight-year-old whines, "How much longer?" even though you've only made it past the parking lot. The teenager drags her feet, glaring at her phone, which has no service, a tragedy she treats like a death in the family.

Your partner says, "This will be good exercise."
You reply, "So would leaving you here."

The Trail Hazards

- Mosquitoes treat your children like an all-you-can-eat buffet.
- The toddler discovers mud and treats it like a spa treatment.
- The eight-year-old insists on collecting rocks the size of bowling balls.
- The teenager announces she saw a bug and demands evacuation.

By the halfway point, your shoulders ache from carrying the toddler, your water is gone, and you're sweating so much you look like you ran a marathon through soup.

Scene: The Beach Day

Maybe hiking wasn't your thing, so you try the beach. This is worse.

The toddler eats sand like it's his new favorite snack. The eight-year-old builds a sandcastle, cries when it collapses, rebuilds it, cries again. The teenager refuses sunscreen, then spends the rest of the day complaining about being "burnt alive."

You lugged six towels, four chairs, an umbrella, and enough snacks to feed an army. None of it makes anyone happy. Meanwhile, the ocean is trying to murder your toddler every time he waddles too close.

Your partner floats on a raft, looking like he's at Club Med. You fantasize about popping it with a seashell.

Scene: The Boat Ride

Someone suggested a boat trip. They were a liar.

The toddler screams the moment he sees a life vest. The eight-year-old gets seasick and vomits Goldfish crackers over the side. The teenager declares, "This is boring," and stares dramatically at the horizon like she's in a music video.

You spend the whole trip clutching snacks, sunscreen, and your sanity, praying no one falls overboard. By the end, the toddler is asleep, the eight-year-old is green, and you have permanent sea legs while your partner says, "That was refreshing."

PRO TIPS: Surviving Outdoor "Fun"

1. Lower the bar. Aim for a walk, not a hike. Aim for thirty minutes, not three hours. If you get longer, it's a miracle.
2. Overpack sunscreen. You will still miss a spot. That spot will blister. Accept it.
3. Snacks double as bribes. Energy bars, gummy bears, whatever works. They are the only currency kids respect outdoors.

4. Bug spray is not optional. Without it, your kids will look like they have medieval plague symptoms.

5. Never trust weather apps. It will rain. It will always rain. Bring ponchos.

By the time you return to your lodging, you are sunburned, sandy, bug-bitten, and emotionally drained.

The kids collapse in front of screens, happy at last.
Your partner says, "That was fun, we should do it again."

You stare at him, skin peeling, and whisper, "Over my dead body."

Part 5: *The Souvenir Shakedown*

Over your dead body. That's what you swore. No more activities. No more money pits.

And then you hit the gift shop.

Scene: The Gift Shop Meltdown

The second you cross the threshold, your children turn into predators who smell weakness. Their pupils dilate. Their hands reach. Their voices rise.

The toddler clutches a stuffed dolphin bigger than his torso.
The eight-year-old demands a glitter snow globe.
The teenager scoffs at the T-shirts, then quietly picks up a $48 hoodie.

You try reason.
You try logic.
You say things like, "We don't need this."

They hear: "Please scream louder."

The Emotional Mugging

Souvenir shops are designed to break parents. The aisles are narrow. The lights are fluorescent. The music is jaunty but threatening.

Your children know this. They weaponize it.

The toddler goes limp on the floor, clutching the dolphin like he's been shot.
The eight-year-old begins to cry, whispering, "You never let me have anything."
The teenager mutters, "This trip sucks," loud enough for strangers to hear.

Now you look like the villain. The other parents in the store nod knowingly, silently chanting, *Give in. Give in.*

The Purchase

You cave. Of course you cave.

You buy the dolphin, the snow globe, and the hoodie. The total is $136. The cashier says, "Do you want a bag?" You want to scream, "Do you want my soul?" but you just nod.

The toddler drops the dolphin in the parking lot and forgets about it.
The snow globe shatters in the hotel room.
The teenager declares the hoodie "shrunk weird" after one wash.

And yet, somehow, you know you'll do it again tomorrow.

PRO TIPS: Surviving the Souvenir Trap

1. Set a budget. Give each kid their own small amount of money to spend however they want. It teaches "responsibility." Mostly it just limits your financial bleeding.

2. Say no early. If you wait until the tantrum starts, you've already lost.
3. Pre-buy cheap souvenirs. Glow sticks, keychains, small plushies. Pull them out like magic when kids start begging.
4. Photographs > junk. Kids forget trinkets, but a ridiculous photo of them mid-meltdown? Priceless.
5. Accept at least one purchase. Fighting every battle will kill you. Pick one, surrender gracefully, and move on.

You trudge out of the gift shop, wallet lighter, bags heavier, children temporarily pacified.

Your partner says, "At least they're happy."

You stare at the receipt and whisper, "Not for long."

Chapter 7: *Eating Out — Restaurants Are Just Battlefields With Menus*

Part 1: *The Myth of Dining Out*

Not for long. Because the receipt is only the appetizer in the feast of regret that is family dining.

Every parent has the fantasy. A nice meal, everyone sitting together, enjoying food and conversation. Maybe even a glass of wine for you, laughter around the table, and a toddler quietly coloring while you savor pasta in peace.

That fantasy dies the second you walk into a restaurant with children.

Scene: The Restaurant Reality

The hostess looks up. She sees your group. She does not smile. She points toward the worst table in the building — the one by the bathroom door or under the freezing vent.

The toddler immediately tries to crawl under the table. The eight-year-old argues over which chair is hers. The teenager announces, "I'm not even hungry." Your partner looks around and says, "This place is nice," which is code for "This will bankrupt us."

The server arrives with forced cheer. The toddler grabs the menu and licks it. The eight-year-old asks, "Do they have pizza?" They do not. She begins to cry. The teenager scrolls through the menu, sighs dramatically, and says, "Ugh, there's nothing here."

You haven't even ordered drinks yet.

The Sensory Nightmare

Restaurants are not designed for children. They are designed for chaos. The lighting is too dim for kids to read the kids' menu. The music is too loud for you to hear the server. The table is too small for all the stuff you have dragged along: crayons, wipes, toys, water bottles, and your last shred of patience.

Meanwhile, every eye in the restaurant is on you. You can feel the collective prayer: "Please let them behave." You already know the answer.

The Parent Experience

You try to act normal. You glance at the wine list. You say, "Maybe I'll get a glass." Your toddler yells, "Juice!" loud enough for the bartender to flinch. The eight-year-old begins stabbing the butter packet with a fork. The teenager asks if she can go outside to "get better reception."

You nod politely at other diners, apologizing with your eyes. Then you wonder why you didn't just eat in the hotel room with microwaved mac and cheese.

PRO TIPS: Lowering the Mythical Bar

1. Pick kid-friendly, not Instagram-worthy. Nobody cares if it has exposed brick and craft cocktails. Go where the chicken nuggets flow freely.
2. Arrive early. Before the dinner rush, before everyone is tired, before your toddler morphs into a gremlin.
3. Know your exit. Always locate the bathroom, the back door, and the fastest way to leave when someone melts down.
4. Bring distractions. Coloring books, tablets, small toys. Silence the judgment of strangers. They are not the ones keeping your child from drinking ketchup straight from the bottle.
5. Order quickly. Do not browse the menu. Do not savor. The longer you wait, the higher the odds of destruction.

By the time drinks arrive, you already know the truth: family dining is not about food or relaxation. It is a public endurance test where you pray no one bleeds.

Part 2: *The Hostess Gauntlet*

It is a public endurance test where you pray no one bleeds. And you haven't even made it past the hostess stand.

Scene: Arrival

You arrive at the restaurant like an invading army. One stroller, two backpacks, three cranky children, and the thousand-yard stare of parents who have already lost.

The hostess greets you with a smile so thin it could slice glass. She sees your stroller and immediately scans the floor plan like she is plotting a military evacuation.

"Table for five?" she asks, as if hoping you'll say, "Just kidding, we'll eat in the car."

The Walk of Shame

You follow her through the restaurant. This is not walking. This is a parade of judgment.

The toddler screams, "I'm hungry!" while dragging his blanket across the floor like a filthy parade flag.
The eight-year-old swings her jacket, narrowly missing three diners.
The teenager stomps along in exaggerated misery, sighing so loudly other tables turn to look.

You smile apologetically as you bump chairs with the stroller. You say, "Sorry, sorry," like it's a mantra. Strangers nod politely but their eyes say, *Why did you bring them here?*

The Stroller Situation

There is no good place for a stroller. The hostess parks it in the aisle, where it immediately becomes an OSHA violation. Servers glare as they attempt to carry trays past it. At least one man in a polo shirt mutters, "This is ridiculous."

You consider folding the stroller. But folding a stroller in public is like performing advanced origami under pressure. You sweat, you curse, you nearly lose a finger. Finally, you wedge it against the wall, praying it does not roll into another diner's soup.

The Table of Doom

The hostess seats you at the worst table in the building. Always.

It will be next to the bathroom, where you can enjoy the soundtrack of flushing toilets.

Or under the AC vent, where your toddler shivers dramatically and declares, "I'm freezing to death."

Or right in the center of the dining room, where your family's chaos can be observed by all, like a zoo exhibit.

You sit down, already sticky with sweat and shame.

The High Chair Battle

The high chair arrives. It looks like it was last cleaned during the Bush administration. You wipe it down with seventeen baby wipes, still uncertain if it's safe. The toddler resists, arching his back like a possessed gymnast. Diners glance over, eyebrows raised, as if you're trying to seat a feral raccoon.

Eventually he's strapped in, glaring at you, plotting revenge.

The Judging Diners

Restaurants are full of silent jurors.

> **The Retired Couple:** Glaring because they were hoping for a quiet night.
>
> **The Business Traveler:** Glaring because he believes his $28 steak entitles him to silence.
>
> **The Young Couple on a Date:** Glaring because your toddler ruined their "romantic vibe."

Other Parents: Not glaring. They smile knowingly, with eyes that say, *Good luck, soldier.*

You sip your water, pretending you don't care. Inside, you are praying for the food to arrive before the toddler discovers the salt shaker.

PRO TIPS: Surviving the Hostess Gauntlet

1. Request corner seating. The farther you are from the action, the fewer glares you'll endure.
2. Lose the stroller early. Park it outside if possible. If not, accept that it is now a permanent tripping hazard.
3. High chair wipes are essential. You will find dried ketchup from the early 2000s.
4. Bring entertainment immediately. Do not wait. Hand over crayons or a tablet the second you sit down.
5. Smile like a lunatic. A big, manic grin disarms at least half the judging strangers.

You glance around the table. The toddler is banging a spoon against the high chair. The eight-year-old is complaining that the chair is "too hard." The teenager is already asking for Wi-Fi.

Your partner opens the menu and says, "This place looks great."

You stare at him, clutching your glass of water like a lifeline.

The gauntlet has only just begun.

Part 3: *The Menu Wars*

The gauntlet has only just begun. And now the menus arrive.

Scene: Ordering Disaster

The toddler grabs the kids' menu and immediately rips it in half. He then uses the crayon to scribble directly on the table. The eight-year-old peers at the options, frowning.

"I don't like grilled cheese."

"Yes, you do."

"No, I don't."

This is a lie. Grilled cheese is her favorite food. But not here. Not today.

The teenager sighs dramatically, flipping through the menu like it personally offended her.

"There's nothing vegan."

You reply, "You're not vegan."

She replies, "Well, maybe I should be."

Your partner, unbothered, says, "I'm getting the steak."

The Expensive Betrayal

Children have a supernatural ability to locate the most expensive item on the menu. It doesn't matter if it's lobster ravioli, truffle pasta, or a $29 steak burger. They will point to it and say, "I want that."

You gently redirect. "How about chicken fingers?"

Cue meltdown.

Now the toddler is screaming "Nuggets!" while the eight-year-old cries that "nothing looks good." The teenager mutters that she'll "just get fries," which you know means she'll eat half your meal later.

Special Requests

When you finally get orders in, they come with demands.

"No cheese."

"Extra cheese."

"Can you cut the crusts off?"

"Can you make it look like the dinosaur nuggets at home?"

The server nods politely, but their eyes scream, *I hate you.*

You say, "Thank you so much," because you are desperate for kindness, even fake kindness, at this point.

Scene: The Drink Disaster

The drinks arrive.
The toddler immediately spills juice down his shirt.
The eight-year-old fills her water with three sugar packets, stirs it, takes one sip, and says, "It's gross."
The teenager orders a Diet Coke, then announces she wanted Sprite.

Your water sits untouched because you are too busy blotting the toddler with napkins that smell faintly of bleach.

The Parent Dilemma

You order something you don't even want because you know you won't be eating it. You'll be eating leftover nuggets, cold fries, and the corner of a quesadilla that mysteriously tastes like Play-Doh.

Your partner says, "I'm starving," and orders an appetizer. You look at him like he just declared bankruptcy.

PRO TIPS: Winning the Menu Wars

1. Steer early. Suggest options before they see the menu. "I think the spaghetti looks good" plants the seed.
2. Stick to familiar foods. Vacations are not the time to introduce shrimp tacos.
3. Order for speed. The first food that hits the table is the only thing preventing a meltdown. Fries are currency.
4. Share meals. Portions are huge. Split something. It saves money and lowers waste when kids inevitably abandon ship.
5. Pack backups. Emergency granola bars in your bag can save the night if the restaurant fails.

The menus are collected. The orders are in. You take a deep breath, praying to the gods of food service.

And then the toddler looks up, sweet and innocent, and says, "I have to pee."

Part 4: *The Waiting Game*

And then the toddler looks up, sweet and innocent, and says, "I have to pee."

You scoop him up and make the trek to the bathroom, weaving through tables, apologizing to strangers as he yells, "I'M PEEING!" the entire way. By the time you return, your water glass is empty, the crayons are broken, and the teenager is face-first in her phone.

The food has not arrived. And you are entering the most dangerous part of the restaurant experience: the waiting game.

Scene: Minute 5

The toddler bangs his fork on the table like a war drum. The eight-year-old asks, "When's the food coming?" The teenager sighs, "This is taking forever."

You remind everyone that it's only been five minutes. They glare at you like you personally delayed the order.

Minute 10

The toddler dumps sugar packets into his water, creating a gritty potion he proudly calls "juice soup." The eight-year-old is lying under the table, announcing loudly, "I live here now." The teenager announces, "I'm going to starve."

You flag down the server, who says cheerfully, "Your food will be right out." This is a lie.

Minute 15

The toddler throws a crayon across the room. It hits a man in a polo shirt, who turns and glares. You mouth, "Sorry!" while dying inside.

The eight-year-old discovers the salt and pepper shakers. She unscrews the tops. You catch her just before disaster strikes. She wails, "You never let me have fun!"

The teenager mutters, "This place is the worst." You resist the urge to remind her she said the same thing yesterday about the beach.

Minute 20

Your partner suggests, "Let's play a game while we wait." He means *I Spy*. The toddler immediately screams, "I spy poop!" The eight-year-old laughs so hard she nearly falls off her chair. The teenager rolls her eyes so far back you're afraid they'll get stuck.

You sip your water and wonder how much wine you can drink before Child Protective Services gets involved.

The Screen Negotiations

You swore you wouldn't use screens. Vacations were going to be about "connection." But after twenty-three minutes of chaos, you hand over the tablet. The toddler quiets instantly, transfixed by a cartoon pig.

The eight-year-old asks for your phone. She plays a game until the battery dies. She announces this like it's your fault.

The teenager refuses a screen, then stares at the wall in exaggerated misery.

The Strangers' Stares

By this point, the restaurant is divided.

- **Some diners smile knowingly.** They've been here. They salute you silently.
- **Some diners are annoyed.** They believe children should be seen and not heard, preferably in another county.
- **Some diners are childless twenty-somethings.** They look at you like you are living their worst nightmare. You want to shout, "Use protection!"

The Parent Experience

You look at your watch every thirty seconds. You begin hallucinating the smell of food. You imagine tackling the server and eating fries straight from the tray.

Your partner says, "It's not that bad." You grip your knife tightly.

PRO TIPS: Surviving the Wait

1. Order appetizers immediately. Fries, bread, chips — anything that arrives fast buys you silence.
2. Pack distractions. Coloring books, small toys, sticker pads. The sugar packets will not survive otherwise.
3. Divide and conquer. One adult entertains, the other stares silently into the distance, preserving sanity.
4. Set a timer. Tell kids the food will be ready in 15 minutes, even if it takes 30. Children don't understand time. Use this against them.
5. Lower your standards. This is not a meal. This is crisis management in a public setting.

Finally, the server approaches with food. Relief floods your body. You imagine angels singing.

And then the toddler says, "I don't want that."

Part 5: *The Aftermath*

And then the toddler says, "I don't want that."

You close your eyes. You breathe deeply. You remind yourself you are in public and therefore cannot flip the table.

The toddler pushes his plate away, nearly sending it into your lap. The eight-year-old picks at her food, eats three fries, and declares she's full. The teenager takes two bites, mutters, "This isn't good," and retreats into her phone.

Your partner eats happily, cleaning every plate within reach. "At least it won't go to waste," he says, as if inhaling a $19 kids' mac and cheese is heroic.

Scene: The Table

By the end, the table looks like a crime scene.

- Napkins crumpled, stained with ketchup and tears.
- Crayons snapped into colorful shrapnel.
- Half-eaten nuggets, abandoned like battlefield casualties.
- A puddle of apple juice slowly seeping toward your lap.

The server approaches, smiling politely, but their eyes scream, *Why do you hate me?* You tip heavily, not out of generosity but out of guilt.

The Check Arrives

The server drops the bill like it's a grenade.

You open it. Your eyes water. $128. Forty of that is fries. You wonder how many groceries you could have bought instead. You briefly consider washing dishes in the back to offset the shame.

Your partner shrugs. "Not too bad." You glare at him so hard his steak nearly digests twice.

The Cruel Twist

You gather your things, wipe sticky hands, wrestle the toddler back into the stroller, and make your exit. You are exhausted. You are broke. You are covered in ketchup.

As you step into the parking lot, the toddler says, "I'm hungry."
The eight-year-old says, "Can we get ice cream?"
The teenager says, "Can we get drive-thru instead?"

You stare at them, hollow-eyed, and wonder if this is what hell feels like.

PRO TIPS: Managing the Aftermath

1. Budget double. Whatever you think dinner will cost, double it. You'll always be right.
2. Tip like a saint. Your server deserves hazard pay.
3. Don't expect leftovers. Kids will abandon food. Partners will eat everything else. Accept that you will leave hungry.
4. Pack snacks anyway. You'll need them on the way home when everyone declares they're starving again.
5. Skip the guilt. Everyone suffers through restaurant meals with kids. It is not you. It is universal law.

You finally collapse into your hotel bed, wallet empty, children sticky, your soul broken.

Your partner smiles and says, "That wasn't so bad."

You stare at him, and for the hundredth time this trip, consider divorce.

Chapter 8: *Sleeping In — The Greatest Vacation Lie*

Part 1: *The Dream vs. The Alarm Clock Child*

You stare at him, and for the hundredth time this trip, consider divorce. But then you think, *Tomorrow will be different. Tomorrow, we'll all sleep in.*

This is the lie you tell yourself as you collapse into bed. The fantasy is intoxicating. You imagine waking at nine, sunlight streaming through the curtains, the smell of coffee in the air. You picture yourself stretching luxuriously while your children are still asleep, angels in their little beds.

You are a fool.

Scene: The Morning Reality

5:32 a.m. The toddler sits up in bed like a possessed doll and yells, "IS IT MORNING YET?"

5:34. The eight-year-old announces she had a bad dream about a unicorn. She climbs into your bed, elbows flying, stealing the blanket.

5:37. The toddler decides he is starving. He screams, "I want cereal!" so loudly that the walls shake.

5:45. The teenager rolls over, covers her head with a pillow, and groans, "Why are you people so loud?"

5:48. Your partner snores, blissfully unaware.

The Parent's Fantasy Dies

You beg them. "Please, go back to sleep. It's still early."

The toddler laughs maniacally. The eight-year-old insists it feels like daytime. The teenager mutters, "I'm never having kids."

By 6:00 a.m., you are fully awake, rummaging through the snack bag, handing out stale granola bars like peace offerings. This is not rest. This is hostage negotiation.

The Crushing Irony

At home, you have to drag them out of bed for school. They act like waking up at 7:30 is medieval torture. But on vacation, their internal clocks shift. Suddenly, dawn is their favorite time of day.

You watch them bouncing on the hotel beds at sunrise, screaming "I'M A JEDI!" while you sip bad coffee and wonder why you paid thousands of dollars to suffer in a different zip code.

PRO TIPS: Surviving the Early Wake-Up

1. Pack breakfast snacks. Mini cereal boxes, granola bars, fruit. Hand them food immediately to buy yourself 15 more minutes.
2. Designate one morning parent. Take turns. One suffers while the other pretends to sleep. Fair is fair.
3. Use blackout curtains. Hotels have them. Close them tight. Sunlight is the enemy.
4. Introduce "quiet time." It won't work, but saying the words makes you feel better.
5. Accept reality. Children are alarm clocks you cannot snooze. Lower expectations and plan for naps later.

By 7:00 a.m., the toddler is sticky, the eight-year-old has lost a sock, the teenager is still in bed threatening to move out, and you have aged ten years.

Vacation sleeping in is not real. It is a myth whispered by parents who lie.

Part 2: *Hotel Beds Are Trampolines, Apparently*

Vacation sleeping in is not real. It is a myth whispered by parents who lie.

And yet, somehow, at 6:45 a.m., your children find new energy reserves. Not for sleeping. For jumping.

Scene: The Morning Trampoline Incident

You are clinging to the edge of the hotel bed, trying to pretend you're asleep. Your toddler climbs onto the mattress and launches himself into the air.

"CANNONBALL!"

He lands directly on your ribcage. You wheeze like you've been tackled by a linebacker.

The eight-year-old joins in, bouncing higher and higher, chanting, "I'm flying! I'm flying!" She is not flying. She is headbutting the headboard.

The teenager pulls a pillow over her head and groans, "This is abuse."

Your partner rolls over, mumbles, "They're just having fun," and goes back to sleep.

The Physics of Pain

Hotel beds are not built for comfort. They are built to withstand jumping children. The springs creak, the mattress groans, and every leap sends shockwaves through your spine.

At one point, the toddler lands on your stomach with both knees. You see your ancestors.

The eight-year-old accidentally kicks over the bedside lamp. It crashes to the floor. You pray housekeeping doesn't charge extra.

The Parent's Perspective

You say, "Stop jumping!"
They laugh and jump higher.

You say, "Someone is going to get hurt!"

The toddler immediately smacks his head on the nightstand.

Cue tears. Cue wailing. Cue judgmental looks from the neighboring room as if you are running an underground daycare.

The Inevitable Chaos

Within ten minutes:

> The toddler is crying, clutching his knee.
>
> The eight-year-old is crying, insisting it was "an accident."
>
> The teenager is crying, because she still isn't awake and "this is the worst vacation ever."

You are crying too, but only on the inside.

PRO TIPS: Hotel Bed Survival

1. Bring a travel mattress or inflatable bed. Give kids their own spot to destroy.
2. Stack pillows on the floor. Someone will fall. Better to land on cushions than tile.
3. Morning screens are worth it. Hand over the tablet. Prevent hospital visits.
4. Consider coffee first. Do not attempt discipline before caffeine. It will end badly.
5. Accept at least one injury. Every trip has a bruise, a scraped knee, or a bumped head. Add it to the vacation scrapbook.

By 8:00 a.m., the beds are unmade, the lamp is broken, the toddler is sticky, and you are Googling "is there wine in the minibar."

Your partner stretches, yawns, and says, "I slept great."

You plot his murder with the broken lamp.

Part 3: *Teenagers, the Opposite Problem*

You plot his murder with the broken lamp. But before you can act, a new battle begins: the teenager.

Toddlers wake before sunrise, bouncing on beds. Teenagers are the opposite. They sleep like the dead. Nothing wakes them. Not light, not noise, not the toddler screaming "I AM A JEDI!" at 6:30 in the morning.

If toddlers are alarm clocks, teenagers are blackout curtains.

Scene: The Wake-Up Attempt

9:00 a.m. The toddler has already eaten two granola bars. The eight-year-old has put on a bathing suit and demanded the pool six times. Your partner is scrolling his phone.

You open the teenager's door. She is cocooned under the covers, hood pulled up, earbuds in. You say, "Time to get up."

She groans.
You say, "We have plans."
She mumbles, "Cancel them."

You consider it.

The Parent's Toolkit

You escalate.

> Step 1: Pull the curtains open. Sunlight floods the room. She hisses like a vampire.
>
> Step 2: Remove the blanket. She yells, "I'm freezing!" and burrows deeper into the fitted sheet.
>
> Step 3: Bribe. "If you get up, we'll stop for iced coffee." She stirs, but does not rise.
>
> Step 4: Threaten. "If you don't get up, no Wi-Fi." This finally works, but at a cost. She emerges snarling, hair wild, muttering curses under her breath.

The Family Conflict

By 9:30 a.m., the toddler is sticky, the eight-year-old is crying because "we're late," and the teenager is sulking, insisting you are ruining her life.

You stand in the middle of the hotel room, clutching sunscreen, wondering why you thought "family vacation" would be relaxing.

Your partner says, "She just needs time to wake up." You reply, "So does a coma patient."

The Emotional Math

Here's the cruel arithmetic:

> Little kids wake too early.
>
> Teenagers wake too late.
>
> Parents wake all the time, never rested.

There is no overlap, no magical sweet spot where everyone wakes naturally at the same time. Either you're up at dawn with toddlers or wasting half the day dragging teenagers out of bed like hostages.

Either way, you lose.

Scene: The Breakfast Deadline

10:01 a.m. Hotel breakfast closed at 10:00. The toddler is wailing for waffles. The eight-year-old is demanding orange juice. The teenager is still glaring at you, holding iced coffee like a protest sign.

You serve dry cereal from a plastic cup while muttering, "This is fine. Everything's fine."

PRO TIPS: Managing the Teenage Sleep Cycle

1. Pick your battles. Not every morning needs to start early. Schedule late activities if possible.
2. Use Wi-Fi as leverage. Cruel but effective. Teens will rise for the promise of connectivity.
3. Bribe strategically. Coffee, smoothies, shopping stops — whatever drags them upright.
4. Stagger activities. Let teens sleep while younger kids swim or play. Saves sanity.
5. Accept the divide. They will never match the toddlers' schedule. Stop expecting harmony.

By 11:00 a.m., everyone is dressed. The toddler has eaten three breakfasts. The eight-year-old is already sunburned. The teenager is wearing sunglasses indoors, sighing loudly with every step.

Your partner says, "That wasn't so bad."

You grab your bag and think, *Next time I'm vacationing alone.*

Part 4: *The Breakfast Deadline Panic*

Next time I'm vacationing alone. But for now, you are sprinting against the cruellest villain of all: the hotel breakfast cut-off.

Scene: The Countdown

9:22 a.m. Breakfast ends at 10:00. You've got 38 minutes. Plenty of time, you think.

9:24. The toddler is naked, running in circles, yelling, "I don't like pants!"

9:27. The eight-year-old insists she has "nothing to wear." You point at her suitcase, bursting with clothes. She bursts into tears.

9:31. The teenager is still in bed, muttering, "It's too early." You threaten to dump water on her. She replies, "Do it. I dare you."

9:35. Your partner is shaving. Shaving. As if this is a spa retreat.

The Descent Into Madness

By 9:40, the toddler is half-dressed, the eight-year-old is crying over mismatched socks, and the teenager has emerged in pyjamas, insisting she's "not hungry."

You yell, "Let's go!" The toddler disappears under the bed. The teenager rolls her eyes so hard you worry about permanent damage. Your partner says, "Relax, there's still time." You fantasize about divorce lawyers.

Scene: The Buffet

9:55 a.m. You make it. Barely. The breakfast room is chaos. Parents sprinting, kids crying, the waffle iron smoking ominously. The staff is already shutting things down, giving you the look reserved for latecomers who think rules don't apply.

The toddler grabs a fistful of muffins and drops them on the floor. The eight-year-old demands waffles, but the machine beeps, stuck in waffle purgatory. The teenager pours herself coffee, takes one sip, and declares it "disgusting."

You settle for cold scrambled eggs that taste like sadness.

The Cruelty of Hotel Breakfast

Hotel breakfasts are a scam. The fruit is always slightly mushy. The bagels are stale. The yogurt is room temperature. And yet, you fight for it. Because it is "free."

You spend the entire meal yelling "Sit down! Don't spill that! Stop licking the jelly packets!" until you realize you haven't eaten a single bite.

PRO TIPS: Winning the Breakfast Battle

1. Plan ahead. Lay out clothes the night before. It won't help, but you'll feel organized.
2. Arrive early. Not "right before they close." Early. Toddlers are awake anyway.
3. Divide forces. One adult corrals kids, the other raids the buffet like a Navy SEAL.
4. Pack extras. Grab fruit, muffins, or cereal boxes to survive the rest of the day.
5. Accept mediocrity. It's not a gourmet meal. It's fuel. Treat it like a pit stop, not an event.

By 10:05, the staff clears the last trays. Your toddler screams for more muffins. Your eight-year-old sobs over the failed waffle. Your teenager mutters, "I told you this was pointless."

You sip cold coffee, staring at your family, and wonder why you ran a marathon for powdered eggs.

Part 5: *The Broken Promise of "Rest"*

You sip cold coffee, staring at your family, and wonder why you ran a marathon for powdered eggs.

This is not rest. This is war.

And yet, every year, you tell yourself, "This vacation will be relaxing. We'll get some sleep. We'll recharge." This is the great broken promise of parenthood. Sleep is gone, replaced by chaos in new locations.

Scene: Afternoon Collapse

By 2:00 p.m., the toddler is asleep in the stroller, head lolling dramatically. The eight-year-old is cranky, crying about nothing and everything. The teenager is yawning, claiming she is "literally dying" from exhaustion.

You? You are walking like a zombie, fuelled by bad coffee and resentment. Your partner says, "Why don't you nap when they nap?" You consider divorce again, then murder, then both.

Of course you cannot nap. Someone has to guard the toddler from rolling into traffic, stop the eight-year-old from shoplifting keychains, and monitor the teenager's Wi-Fi negotiations.

The Evening Illusion

Dinner ends. The kids are allegedly "tired." You think, *Finally, an early night.*

At 8:00 p.m., the toddler is bouncing on the bed singing "Baby Shark."
At 8:15, the eight-year-old is sobbing because she forgot her stuffed animal at home.
At 8:30, the teenager insists she cannot possibly sleep without charging her phone first.

By 9:00, your partner is snoring. By 9:15, you are googling "silent retreats" and wondering how much flights to anywhere cost.

The Parents' Myth

Parents chase the idea of "rest" like explorers chase El Dorado. It is rumored to exist. It is never found.

Every brochure, every Instagram post, every smug parent who says, "We had such a relaxing trip" is lying. They are either childless, drugged, or faking it for likes.

The truth is simple: vacations with kids are not restful. They are noisy, sticky, exhausting, and occasionally hilarious.

PRO TIPS: Coping With the Broken Promise

1. Redefine rest. A five-minute scroll in the bathroom counts. So does lying down with your eyes closed while kids jump on the bed.
2. Nap shifts. Trade off with your partner. One watches kids, one collapses. Fair is fair.
3. Embrace bedtime screens. If thirty minutes of cartoons buys you peace, take it. The American Academy of Pediatrics is not here.
4. Treat sleep like a bonus. If you get it, celebrate. If not, coffee exists.

5. Stop chasing perfection. The chaos is the memory. Nobody remembers being well-rested. They remember screaming about waffles at 9:58 a.m.

The Darkly Funny Hope

By the end of the trip, you are ragged. You are tired. You are sticky. And yet, when you look back, you will not remember every sleepless morning. You will remember the toddler's ridiculous hotel-bed cannonballs, the eight-year-old's dramatic waffle meltdown, the teenager's sulky sunglasses at breakfast.

You will laugh. Eventually. Not now, but someday.

And then, because parents are eternal optimists with short-term memory loss, you will book another trip. You will say, "This time we'll sleep in. This time will be different."

It won't. But hope keeps you going.

Chapter 9: *Family Bonding — Or Mutual Destruction*

Part 1: *The Myth of Family Bonding*

It won't. But hope keeps you going.

Hope is what convinces parents that vacations are about family bonding. You picture smiling group photos, laughter around dinner tables, long walks holding hands. In your mind, it looks like a travel commercial. Everyone is sun-kissed, relaxed, and saying things like, "This is the best vacation ever."

The reality? It's survival mode in matching T-shirts.

Scene: The Morning Bonding Attempt

You announce brightly, "Let's all spend the day together!"

The toddler yells, "No!" and runs off.

The eight-year-old says, "Do I have to?"

The teenager mutters, "Kill me."

Your partner shrugs like this is normal.

You insist. "Come on, it'll be fun." These are the most dangerous words a parent can say.

The Fantasy vs. Reality

> **Fantasy:** Family bike ride along the boardwalk.
> **Reality:** Toddler in meltdown because the helmet is "too round." Teenager refuses to pedal. Someone crashes into a trash can.
>
> **Fantasy:** Family dinner filled with laughter.
> **Reality:** Toddler spills juice. Eight-year-old cries because her food is touching. Teenager refuses to make eye contact with anyone.
>
> **Fantasy:** Family photo at a scenic overlook.
> **Reality:** Toddler picks his nose. Eight-year-old sticks out her tongue. Teenager looks like she's attending a funeral.

You scroll Instagram and see other families looking perfect. You forget that those parents also bribed their kids with ice cream and took 274 photos to get one where no one was crying.

Scene: The Group Outing

You herd the family into a rental car for "quality time."

Five minutes in, the toddler screams because the sun touched his leg. The eight-year-old is furious she didn't get the window seat. The teenager demands the aux cord, then plays music no one else likes.

You shout, "We are making memories!" They shout, "We hate this!"

You grip the steering wheel and whisper, "We will bond if it kills us."

PRO TIPS: Surviving the Myth

1. Lower expectations. Bonding does not look like commercials. It looks like everyone surviving in the same general area.
2. Keep it short. Thirty minutes of togetherness is enough. Longer, and you risk bloodshed.
3. Document chaos. Take the photo even if someone is crying. Those are the real memories.
4. Bribe unapologetically. Ice cream, snacks, or screen time. Nothing bonds kids faster than sugar.
5. Celebrate small wins. Ten minutes without fighting counts as family bonding.

By the end of the day, your toddler is sticky, your eight-year-old is sulking, your teenager is glaring, and your partner is saying, "That wasn't so bad."

You smile, exhausted, and think, *If this is bonding, no wonder families need therapy.*

Part 2: *Car Time — Mobile Cage Match*

If this is bonding, no wonder families need therapy. And nowhere is that truer than in the car.

The car is the great equalizer of family vacations. It's too small, too hot, and too full of snacks ground into the seats. It's where fights begin, alliances shift, and parents lose their will to live somewhere between Exit 42 and "Are we there yet?"

Scene: The Doomed Drive

You load the car with military precision. Snacks packed. Drinks balanced. Tablets charged. Everyone buckled in. You pull out of the driveway thinking, *This time will be fine.*

It takes three minutes for the chaos to begin.

"Her elbow is touching me!"
"He's looking out my window!"
"Can we stop for ice cream?"

The toddler screams because his Goldfish crackers broke in half. The eight-year-old chants, "Are we there yet?" on repeat. The teenager rolls her eyes, blasts music through her earbuds, and mutters, "This family is so toxic."

The Parent's Arsenal

You try games. "Let's play I Spy!" The toddler immediately shouts, "POOP!" and the game ends.

You try music. The toddler demands Baby Shark. The teenager demands rap. The eight-year-old sings Frozen at full volume. Everyone is furious.

You try snacks. Within seconds, crumbs cover the backseat. Someone spills juice. Someone else claims their snack is smaller than everyone else's.

Finally, you threaten. "If you don't stop, I'll turn this car around!" This is a lie. You've already prepaid for the hotel. There is no turning back.

Scene: The Shuttle Bus

If it's not your car, it's worse.

You pile onto a crowded shuttle bus to the airport or theme park. The toddler screams because he wants the blue seat. The eight-year-old kicks the back of a stranger's chair. The teenager refuses to sit with the family, retreating to the farthest possible seat while glaring at her phone.

Everyone around you watches like they're at a live performance of *Lord of the Flies*. You whisper apologies while silently plotting your own escape.

The Backseat Dynamics

The backseat is not a place for bonding. It is a war zone.

> **Personal space disputes:** "She's breathing my air!"
>
> **Window fights:** "That's MY side!"
>
> **Temperature wars:** One child is sweating, the other is freezing, the teenager says the AC "feels cheap."
>
> **Silent sabotage:** Someone passes gas, blames someone else, and chaos erupts.

You grip the steering wheel, white-knuckled, and wonder how long before you can legally eject passengers.

The Parent Experience

You keep your eyes on the road, muttering, "Just fifteen more minutes." Fifteen becomes thirty. Thirty becomes an eternity.

Your partner says, "It's not that bad." You glare so hard he almost drives off the road.

At some point, you blast the radio just to drown out the noise. No one sings along. No one bonds. You sit in silence, praying for a traffic jam just so you can pull over and cry in peace.

PRO TIPS: Surviving Mobile Cage Match

1. Assign seats. Do not negotiate. Dictatorship works better than democracy in the backseat.
2. Noise-cancelling headphones. For you, not them. Save your sanity.
3. Pack double snacks. They will compare. They will fight. Eliminate excuses.
4. Divide entertainment. Tablets, books, music. Each child in their own world is the dream.
5. Keep drives short. Anything over two hours is a death sentence. Plan stops, stretch legs, and pretend it's part of the itinerary.

By the time you arrive, the car is a landfill, the toddler is sticky, the eight-year-old is pouting, the teenager is furious, and you are whispering, "Never again."

And yet, deep down, you know tomorrow you'll load them back in, snacks packed, ready to try again.

Because apparently parents are masochists.

Part 3: *Pool Time Politics*

Because apparently parents are masochists. Which is why, despite everything, you now find yourself at the hotel pool.

You dreamed of this. A sunny afternoon, lounging in a chair, drink in hand, maybe even reading a book. The kids splashing happily, laughter echoing, the picture of family vacation bliss.

The dream dies the moment sunscreen enters the chat.

Scene: The Sunscreen Wars

You announce, "Time for sunscreen!" The toddler immediately runs. The eight-year-old groans, "It's sticky!" The teenager rolls her eyes and mutters, "I don't even burn."

You chase the toddler around the pool deck, slipping like Bambi on ice, while other parents nod in solidarity. You bribe the eight-year-old with promises of ice cream. The teenager refuses until you hiss, "Fine, but when you're red as a lobster, don't complain."

By the time everyone is coated, you are sweating, covered in white streaks, and smell like a coconut crime scene.

Scene: The Pool Politics

The toddler leaps straight in without floaties, nearly giving you a heart attack. You haul him out, strap him in, and he screams, "I don't like this!"

The eight-year-old grabs the only pool noodle and declares it her personal property. The toddler screams for it. The fight escalates until you threaten to confiscate all floaties.

The teenager sits at the edge, scrolling her phone, loudly declaring, "This is so boring." Then she dips a toe in and shrieks, "It's freezing!"

You try to sit in a chair for one blessed minute. The toddler yells, "WATCH ME!" The eight-year-old yells, "WATCH ME!" The teenager yells, "DON'T WATCH ME!"

Your partner is mysteriously gone. Probably at the bar.

The Parent Experience

You are sweating, your hair is frizzy, and your swimsuit is clinging in places that should not be public. You try to sip a drink, but the toddler demands you swim. The eight-year-old demands you time her handstands. The teenager demands you stop embarrassing her.

You glance longingly at the one parent sitting in a chair reading a book. That parent is not real. That parent is a hologram.

Scene: The Unexpected Bonding

And then, briefly, it works.

The toddler floats happily in his tube. The eight-year-old teaches him how to kick. The teenager, despite herself, laughs when he splashes her. For five whole minutes, everyone is smiling.

It is fragile, fleeting, and perfect. The kind of moment you will remember when you're back home, tired, broke, and unpacking wet swimsuits.

PRO TIPS: Pool Survival

1. Arrive early. Pool toys vanish faster than dignity. Grab chairs before the chaos begins.
2. Bring your own floaties. Avoid the noodle wars by packing backup.
3. Accept sunscreen misery. It's sticky. It's messy. It's non-negotiable.

4. Rotate supervision. One parent in the pool, one parent attempting to sit like a human. Trade off.
5. Embrace the fleeting moments. Even if it's only five minutes, those are the vacation memories that stick.

By the time you pack up, you are sunburned, soaked, and exhausted. But you also caught a glimpse — however brief — of actual family bonding.

It may have come wrapped in sunscreen, sibling fights, and screams, but it was there. And that is enough to keep you going.

Part 4: *Forced Fun Activities*

It may have come wrapped in sunscreen, sibling fights, and screams, but it was there. And that is enough to keep you going.

Which is how you make your biggest mistake yet. You say the cursed words:

"Let's do something fun together."

Scene: The Family Board Game

You set up Monopoly in the hotel room. The toddler immediately eats one of the houses. The eight-year-old cries because she wanted to be the dog piece. The teenager rolls her eyes and says, "This is dumb."

You try to explain the rules. The toddler flips the board. The eight-year-old demands extra money. The teenager "accidentally" cheats.

Ten minutes in, the toddler is crying, the eight-year-old is yelling, the teenager is sulking, and you are regretting every decision that led to this moment.

Your partner says, "This is great family time." You fantasize about throwing him out the window.

Scene: The Family Hike

Maybe a game indoors was the wrong choice. So you try outdoors. Fresh air. Nature. Bonding.

You announce, "We're going on a hike!"

The toddler demands to be carried before you even reach the trailhead. The eight-year-old whines, "My legs hurt." The teenager mutters, "This is literally torture."

You spend the entire hike saying things like, "Watch out for poison ivy," "Don't throw rocks at your sister," and "Yes, we're almost there."

When you finally reach the scenic overlook, you imagine a perfect family photo. The toddler is picking his nose. The eight-year-old is pouting. The teenager is glaring. You snap the photo anyway, because you are desperate for evidence this wasn't a complete waste.

Scene: The Scavenger Hunt

In a final act of desperation, you invent a scavenger hunt. Find a seashell, find a feather, find something blue.

The toddler proudly brings you a cigarette butt. The eight-year-old fights because her feather is "better" than his shell. The teenager sighs, "This is so cringe," and wanders off, ignoring all rules.

You declare a tie just to end it. No one is happy.

The Parent Experience

You wanted smiles. You got chaos. You wanted bonding. You got bruises. You wanted laughter. You got accusations of cheating, whining about bugs, and at least one child crying in public.

And yet, in between the disasters, there are moments. A shared joke. A silly dance. A photo that accidentally looks like joy. Small flashes of connection hidden in the wreckage.

PRO TIPS: Forced Fun Without Full Mutiny

1. Keep it short. Thirty minutes max. Kids treat longer like prison sentences.
2. Pick battles. Not every activity needs to involve everyone. Divide and conquer.
3. Sneak in fun. Don't announce "bonding time." Just hand them cards or start walking. Less pressure, fewer groans.
4. Bribe, always. Ice cream, screen time, pool time. Incentives are your best friend.
5. Save the photo. Even if they're all sulking, snap it. Someday you'll laugh.

By the end, the toddler is sticky, the eight-year-old is sulking, the teenager is glaring, and your partner says, "That was nice."

You stare at him, covered in bug spray and regret, and whisper, "Define nice."

Part 5: *The Accidental Bonding Moments*

"Define nice." That's what you muttered last night. And yet somehow, here you are the next morning, sipping coffee from a flimsy paper cup, watching your kids dissolve into giggles because the toddler just shouted across the hotel lobby, "Daddy farted!"

It isn't the Hallmark moment you pictured. But it is a moment.

Scene: The Poolside Collapse

The pool has been chaos all afternoon. There's been screaming, splash fights, sunscreen in your eyes, and at least one meltdown about goggles. But then, as the sun starts to dip, the toddler finally crashes in your lap. He's damp, warm, and completely out, drooling onto your shoulder.

The eight-year-old wraps herself in a towel and whispers, "This was fun." The teenager rolls her eyes but sits next to you anyway, scrolling her phone. For ten full minutes, no one is fighting. The sound of the pool fades. It's quiet, and you realize: this is the memory. Not the fights, not the chaos, but this still, sleepy moment.

Scene: The Backseat Truce

The car is a landfill of crumbs and juice boxes. You're halfway back from an exhausting excursion, bracing for another round of "Are we there yet?" when you notice something rare.

The eight-year-old leans her head on her sister's shoulder. The teenager makes a face, but she doesn't push her away. In fact, she pulls the blanket over her sister's legs.

You catch it in the rearview mirror and think, *This is it. This is why I put myself through hell.*

Five minutes later, the toddler snores so loudly the entire car shakes. All three kids are quiet. You almost cry from relief. You almost believe in peace on earth.

Scene: The Hotel Bed Dogpile

Bedtime has been its usual circus: teeth not brushed, pyjamas not packed, everyone fighting over pillows. But then, as exhaustion wins, all three kids collapse on the same bed. The toddler sprawls sideways, the eight-year-old clutches her stuffed animal, and the teenager mutters, "Don't touch me" before promptly falling asleep with her arm draped across her sister.

You climb in beside them, no room left for yourself, half hanging off the bed. Your partner snores already. And yet, somehow, you're smiling in the dark. Because for once, they're all together, and they're quiet, and it feels like love.

Scene: The Unexpected Joke

At a crowded restaurant, everyone is tired and cranky. The toddler is picking at breadsticks, the eight-year-old is pouting, the teenager is texting under the table. You're ready to give up when suddenly the eight-year-old tells a joke. It's not funny, not really, but the toddler laughs so hard he spits water everywhere.

The teenager tries not to laugh, fails, and snorts. You laugh too, mostly out of shock. For the first time that day, you're all laughing together. Strangers stare, but you don't care. Because for that one second, you're not just surviving. You're happy.

The Parent Experience

Here's the truth: the "bonding" you imagine never happens on schedule. It doesn't happen in front of the scenic overlook, or during the carefully planned activity, or in the perfectly posed family photo. Those moments collapse under the weight of expectations.

Real bonding sneaks in sideways. It's the toddler's nonsense songs in the backseat. The eight-year-old's pride when she shows you a seashell. The teenager's sarcastic joke that, against all odds, makes you laugh. Those flashes arrive between tantrums and eye rolls, tucked inside the chaos.

And those are the moments that make it worth it.

PRO TIPS: Spotting the Real Bonding

1. Stop forcing it. The more you plan "togetherness," the more it implodes. Let bonding sneak up.

2. Celebrate small wins. Ten seconds of laughter counts. So does a sibling sharing fries without violence.

3. Notice kindness. A teenager carrying the toddler's floaties, an eight-year-old offering a bite of her snack. These micro-moments are gold.

4. Take the photo anyway. Even if someone's crying, snap it. Those imperfect shots are the ones you'll laugh at later.

5. Let go of the big picture. Vacations aren't epic movies. They're blooper reels with occasional heartwarming cameos.

The Positive Note

By the end of the trip, you're tired, broke, and sticky. You've refereed fights, bribed with ice cream, and considered abandoning everyone at least once. But when you look back later, it won't be the screaming or the spilled juice that rises to the surface.

It'll be the weird jokes, the sleepy backseat snuggles, the laughter that caught you off guard. It'll be the messy, accidental bonding moments you couldn't have planned if you tried.

And those are the moments that remind you: yes, it was worth it.

Chapter 10: *Packing Up — The Final Boss Battle*

Part 1: *The Packing Panic*

And those are the moments that remind you: yes, it was worth it. Until you remember you have to pack.

Packing up at the end of a vacation is the final boss fight of parenting. You survived the meals, the pool meltdowns, the forced fun, the car rides. Now comes the true test: getting everything back into the same bags it came in, on a strict deadline, with children actively sabotaging you.

Scene: The Night-Before Optimism

You make a bold announcement: "Tonight we'll get organized so we're ready for tomorrow."

The toddler immediately empties an entire drawer of clothes onto the floor, shouting, "I HELP!" The eight-year-old begins a scavenger hunt for "special treasures," which includes a half-eaten granola bar and three shells. The teenager lies on the bed and says, "Why bother? We'll just unpack again at home."

Your partner turns on the TV.

So much for organized.

Scene: The Morning Reality

Morning arrives. Checkout is at 11:00. It is 10:07.

You are frantically stuffing socks into shoes and rolling shirts like a desperate TikTok influencer. The toddler keeps running off with the hairbrush. The eight-year-old wails, "I can't find my bathing suit!" even though it's damp and hanging right in front of her face.

The teenager sighs every five minutes, muttering, "This is so stressful," while doing nothing.

You shout, "EVERYONE FIND YOUR SHOES!" The toddler puts on swim fins. The eight-year-old finds one flip-flop. The teenager announces she can't find her sneakers because "someone probably stole them."

You are one sock short, one nerve away from snapping, and one step closer to living in this hotel forever.

The Parent Experience

Packing to go on vacation is easy. Hope carries you. You carefully fold outfits. You color-coordinate. You imagine cute vacation photos.

Packing to leave is chaos. Clothes are dirty. Shoes are missing. Half the toys are broken. Everyone has more souvenirs than will physically fit in the suitcase. It's less "fold and zip" and more "shove and pray."

PRO TIPS: Avoiding Packing Panic

1. Pack early. Start the night before. (You won't. But pretend.)
2. Assign roles. Kids get one task each: find shoes, collect toys, empty drawers. They'll fail, but it keeps them busy.
3. Contain souvenirs. Dedicate one bag to shells, magnets, and other junk. Saves space and sanity.
4. Do a shoe count. Always. If you don't, you'll be at the airport with one Croc.
5. Accept imperfection. Something will be lost. It's cheaper to replace a T-shirt than your sanity.

By 10:58, the suitcases are bulging, the toddler is crying, the eight-year-old is missing her sock, the teenager is sulking, and your partner is saying, "Relax, we've got plenty of time."

You silently plot his destruction as you shove the last flip-flop into your carry-on.

Part 2: *The Suitcase Showdown*

You silently plot his destruction as you shove the last flip-flop into your carry-on. But the real battle hasn't even begun. The suitcases are waiting.

On the way here, packing was an art form. Clothes were rolled neatly. Everything fit like Tetris. You were smug. "Look how efficient we are!"

On the way home, it's survival.

Scene: The First Attempt

You unzip the largest suitcase. It's already bulging. You stuff in T-shirts, swimsuits, and damp towels that smell like seaweed. The zipper groans in protest.

"Mom, can you pack this?" The eight-year-old hands you a plastic bag full of seashells. Not delicate shells. Huge, jagged ones. Some still smell like fish.

"Sweetie, these won't fit."
"They have to! They're my treasure!"

You sigh and wedge them between sneakers. Somewhere in there, a crab claw pokes you in the hand.

Scene: The Toy Smuggling

Meanwhile, the toddler is sneaking toys into the suitcase. A truck. A stuffed giraffe. Half a coloring book. A banana.

You pull them out. He cries like you've cancelled Christmas. You shove the giraffe back in. The banana goes in the trash.

The teenager drags over a shopping bag. "I bought stuff."

You peer inside. Three hoodies, two pairs of shoes, a giant plush sloth. None of it fits.

"Where is this going to go?" you ask.
She shrugs. "Not my problem."

Scene: The Zipper Crisis

The suitcase is now so full it's practically alive. You sit on top of it, grunting, trying to force the zipper shut. The toddler thinks this is hilarious and climbs on your back. The eight-year-old chants, "Push harder!" The teenager films you for Snapchat.

The zipper moves one inch, then jams. You tug. It jams harder. You yank. The zipper snaps clean off.

You sit there, sweaty and broken, while your partner says, "Maybe we should buy another bag."

You picture murdering him with the broken zipper pull.

Scene: The Desperate Fix

You dig through the room. You find a plastic laundry bag. You stuff it full of wet swimsuits and pray it won't split. You tie the handle in seventeen knots.

The teenager complains, "That looks embarrassing."
You hiss, "So does your attitude."

Finally, with a combination of sitting, swearing, and prayer, you get the largest suitcase closed. It bulges ominously, like it might explode mid-air. You pat it like a wild animal, whispering, "Stay."

The Parent Experience

Packing up is not just about luggage. It's about dignity. It's about proving you can shove an impossible amount of junk into a finite space. It's about holding the line when your child insists on bringing home an entire stick they found "for memories."

And weirdly, it's also bonding. You laugh when the suitcase falls over. You laugh when the toddler sneaks in his toy again. You laugh because if you don't, you'll cry.

PRO TIPS: Surviving the Suitcase Showdown

1. Bring a foldable duffel. It will save you when the souvenirs multiply like rabbits.
2. Vacuum bags. Suck the air out of dirty clothes. Just don't forget a way to open them later.
3. Assign limits. One hoodie, one stuffed animal, one "treasure." Anything more stays behind.
4. Pack dirty on top. You'll need laundry first anyway. Saves time at home.
5. Laugh at the chaos. The suitcase will never look like it did on day one. That's not failure. That's proof you had an adventure.

By the end, the suitcases are closed, barely. They look like they've been through war. You are sweaty, sticky, and triumphant.

The toddler claps. The eight-year-old cheers. The teenager mutters, "That's not going to fit in the overhead."

You collapse on the bed, victorious. For now.

Part 3: *The Hotel Room Sweep*

You collapse on the bed, victorious. For now. Because the real enemy is not the suitcase. It's the hotel room.

Hotel rooms are black holes. They eat socks, chargers, and stuffed animals for breakfast. And checkout is the cruel countdown clock forcing you to face it.

Scene: The Countdown

10:15 a.m. Checkout is at 11:00. You say, "Okay, let's just do a quick sweep."

The toddler immediately hides under the bed, refusing to come out. The eight-year-old insists she can't find her flip-flop. The teenager says, "I don't even know what's mine anymore."

You start opening drawers. One has your partner's swimsuit. Another has a half-eaten Pop-Tart. You don't even remember buying Pop-Tarts.

Scene: The Lost and Found Hunt

The toddler yells, "I can't find Giraffey!" This is his stuffed animal, his emotional support system, his best friend. You drop everything. The search is now a life-or-death mission.

You pull back sheets. You lift the mattress. You crawl under the bed and find:

- One sock.
- A LEGO.
- Half a Goldfish cracker.

No Giraffey.

The toddler is sobbing. The eight-year-old is yelling, "You never care about my stuff!" The teenager is lying on the bed scrolling TikTok.

Then, at 10:42, you find Giraffey stuffed inside the minibar fridge. No one knows how he got there. No one asks.

Scene: The Tech Scramble

"Where's my charger?" the teenager demands. You find three chargers, none of which are hers. The toddler insists the remote control is his "toy." The eight-year-old is holding a cord that belongs to no one.

You realize you have lost at least two chargers and possibly a tablet. You briefly consider sacrificing them to the hotel gods.

Scene: The Parent Guilt

At 10:53, you're stuffing random junk into grocery bags. The toddler's sandals. The eight-year-old's bracelet. A hotel pen you don't remember taking.

Housekeeping knocks. You panic. You look around at the destruction: wet towels, crumbs, spilled juice, beds that look like they've been in combat. You leave a tip that is half cash, half apology.

The Parent Experience

The hotel sweep is not about finding things. It's about realizing how much you've lost. Hair ties. Socks. Chargers. Your will to live.

But it's also the moment you see your family's chaos condensed in one space. The laughter, the mess, the toys, the weird snacks. It's all there, proof you were here. Proof you lived.

PRO TIPS: Winning the Hotel Sweep

1. Assign zones. One adult checks the bathroom, one checks the beds, one checks under furniture. Kids do nothing.
2. Bring a bag for "last minute junk." It will be ugly, it will be heavy, but it will save you.
3. Check the fridge. You'll always find something there. Sometimes it's milk. Sometimes it's Giraffey.
4. Count chargers. Do this three times. They multiply and vanish like gremlins.
5. Tip housekeeping well. They saw the battlefield. They deserve combat pay.

By 11:00, you've found the stuffed animal, three socks, two chargers, and your dignity—barely. You zip the last bag, herd the kids into the hallway, and whisper, "We made it."

Then the eight-year-old says, "Wait. Where's my swimsuit?"

Part 4: *The Check-Out Chaos*

"Where's my swimsuit?" she asks at 11:01, as if time is infinite and you aren't already breaking hotel policy by existing. You shove it into the junk bag and march everyone to the elevator.

This is it: the last hurdle. The check-out gauntlet.

Scene: The Lobby Arrival

The elevator doors open, and it's like entering a war zone. Families everywhere. Suitcases piled like barricades. Toddlers crying. Parents with thousand-yard stares.

You shuffle toward the front desk. The toddler drags his suitcase sideways, tripping strangers. The eight-year-old insists on pushing the luggage cart, nearly mowing down a retiree. The teenager slumps against a wall, earbuds in, broadcasting misery.

You clutch the room keys like they're diamonds.

Scene: The Line of Doom

The line is long. Always long. Every parent in front of you is arguing about resort fees. Every child behind you is shrieking. The toddler announces, "I HAVE TO PEE," at top volume. The eight-year-old says she's starving. The teenager groans, "This is taking forever."

You glare at the clock. It's 11:07. Each minute feels like dog years.

Scene: The Lost Key Crisis

When it's finally your turn, you hand over the room keys. The clerk smiles politely. "There should be three."

You have two.

You check your pockets. Your bag. The toddler's diaper bag. The eight-year-old swears she saw it "in the bathroom." The teenager says, "It's probably under the bed," which is not helpful.

You mutter, "Can we just…not?" The clerk smiles wider. "No problem, we'll just charge your card."

You die inside.

Scene: The Lobby Meltdown

While you're signing papers, the toddler lies flat on the floor, starfished in protest. The eight-year-old is fighting with her over a half-eaten granola bar. The teenager is scrolling her phone, sighing theatrically, as if being in public with her family is a human rights violation.

Other guests watch. Some smile knowingly. Some judge. One couple without kids whispers, "Never." You want to shout, "Good. Don't."

Scene: The Parent Guilt

You hand over your keycard wallet and slide a tip to the clerk, even though you already tipped housekeeping. You are riddled with guilt. Did you take too many towels? Did you leave crumbs? Did you traumatize housekeeping with your toddler's crayon masterpiece on the desk?

Probably.

You over-tip. Because guilt is a parent's currency.

The Parent Experience

Check-out is not just logistics. It's a public performance. You're sweaty, overloaded with bags, trying to prove you are a responsible adult while your children act like extras in a disaster movie.

And yet, when you finally roll your luggage out the door, there's relief. You made it. You survived. You even got your deposit back.

PRO TIPS: Conquering Check-Out

1. Prepare the night before. Keys, wallets, junk bag. Do not wait until 10:59.
2. Assign roles. One parent handles the desk. The other wrangles children far, far away.

3. Bribe strategically. Granola bars, lollipops, or screen time will buy you ten blessed minutes in line.

4. Accept fees. You will lose a key. You will get charged. Consider it a "parenting tax."

5. Tip well. It buys forgiveness for the juice stains and the crayon artwork.

By the time you collapse into the shuttle or car, you are drenched in sweat, lighter in wallet, and heavier in stress.

The toddler says, "That was fun." The eight-year-old asks, "When can we come back?" The teenager mutters, "Never again."

You sit back, whispering, "We're done."

Except you're not. There's still the journey home.

Part 5: *The Journey Home*

Except you're not. There's still the journey home.

The true epilogue of every family vacation isn't the beach, the pool, or the overpriced souvenir shops. It's the car ride, shuttle, or flight home — that long stretch of time where everyone crashes, the snacks run out, and, against all odds, you realize it was kind of wonderful.

Scene: The Car Ride Home

You pile into the car. The toddler is sticky with leftover lollipop. The eight-year-old insists she's starving, even though she ate two muffins at checkout. The teenager dramatically announces, "I can't sit in this car for five hours. I'll die."

You nod. "Great. Then we'll bury you at the next rest stop."

Thirty minutes in, the toddler is asleep, head tilted back at an alarming angle. The eight-year-old is half-watching a movie on the tablet, half-singing to herself. The teenager is scrolling quietly. The car is… calm. For the first time all week.

You grip the wheel, sip your gas station coffee, and smile.

Scene: The Flight Home

If you're flying, it's another kind of circus. The toddler insists on kicking the seat in front of him. The eight-year-old spills juice on her shirt. The teenager pretends not to know you.

But then, somewhere over Ohio, the toddler curls into your lap and falls asleep. The eight-year-old leans against your arm. The teenager even takes out an earbud long enough to say, "This wasn't the worst trip."

It's not glamorous. But it's golden.

Scene: The Weird Sentimentality

You glance at your partner. He's dozing off with his mouth open. Your kids are sprawled across you like sweaty, tired puppies. You are cramped, sore, broke, and desperate for silence.

And you think: *I'd do it again.*

That's the parent's curse. You forget the tantrums, the fights, the sunscreen battles. You remember the giggles, the cannonballs, the stupid inside jokes. The disasters fade. The bonding sticks.

The Parent Experience

The journey home is the emotional reset. Kids are calmer, parents are too tired to care, and everyone is quietly marinating in the afterglow of "we actually did this."

It's messy. It's exhausting. It's perfect in its own broken way.

PRO TIPS: Making the Journey Home Less Miserable

1. Pack car/plane snacks separately. Fresh stash for the ride. Prevents mutiny.
2. Embrace screen time. The rules are gone. Let them binge. Survival > limits.
3. Schedule silence. Headphones for everyone, even you. Blessed quiet.
4. Capture reflections. Ask, "What was your favorite part?" The answers will surprise you.
5. Plan recovery time. Don't schedule a dentist appointment the morning after you get home. You need one day to stare at laundry and question your life.

The Positive Note

By the time you pull into your driveway, unload the car, or stumble out of the airport, you are drained. The house feels too quiet. The laundry pile looks like Everest. And yet, the kids are already asking, "When can we go again?"

And the wild thing is… you're already thinking about it too. Because despite the tantrums, the packing panic, the lobby meltdowns, and the crushed granola bars in your bag, there was magic. Messy, chaotic, loud magic.

Vacations with kids aren't relaxing. They aren't neat. But they are unforgettable.

And in the end, that's why we keep going.

Conclusion: *Why We Keep Going*

Vacations with kids are not restful. They are not serene. They do not involve cocktails by the pool while your children play quietly like background extras in a commercial.

They are loud. Sticky. Exhausting. Full of sunscreen fights, lost shoes, car ride meltdowns, and the never-ending hunt for a stuffed animal named Giraffey. They will drain your bank account, your patience, and your will to live.

And yet.

They're also magic.

Not the kind of magic that looks good on Instagram. Real magic. The toddler's goofy cannonball. The eight-year-old's dramatic waffle meltdown that will make you laugh for years. The teenager's sarcastic joke that accidentally brings the whole family together.

It's the messy, unpredictable, unfiltered moments that stick. The unplanned giggles. The sleepy backseat snuggles. The late-night hotel dogpile when everyone passes out in one bed.

That's the truth about family vacations: the chaos fades, the memories stay.

Your Takeaway as a Mom

- You are not failing when your kids fight in the car. You are normal.
- You are not failing when the pool sunscreen ends in tears. You are normal.
- You are not failing when you pack wrong, lose a charger, or bribe with ice cream. You are surviving — and that's winning.

Because your kids won't remember the tantrums. They'll remember the giggles. They won't remember the lobby meltdowns. They'll remember the goofy inside jokes. They won't remember that you lost your mind in the car. They'll remember that you were there. Together.

The Positive Note

So, yes — vacations with kids are chaos. They are loud. They are sticky. They are exhausting.

And they are the greatest gift you'll give your kids.

Because when they're grown, they won't look back and say, "Remember how well-organized Mom was?" They'll say, "Remember when we all laughed so hard Dad spit soda through his nose?"

That's the magic. That's why we keep going.

So unpack the laundry, pour yourself a giant cup of coffee (or wine), and start planning the next one.

Because you're a mom. And that's what moms do.

Coming Soon in the *For Mommies* Series

Vacations for Mommies — Surviving Family Getaways Without Losing Your Mind

Holidays for Mommies — Wrapping, Cooking, and Crying in the Pantry

Dieting for Mommies — Because Cake for Breakfast Still Counts

Fashion for Mommies — Yoga Pants, Again?

Dating for Mommies — Swiping With Snacks in Your Hair

Sports for Mommies — Sidelines, Snacks, and Silent Screaming

School for Mommies — Homework, PTA, and Lunchbox Battles

Toddlers for Mommies — Sticky, Loud, and Up Too Early

Teens for Mommies — Eye-Rolls Are a Love Language

Birthday Parties for Mommies — Balloons, Sugar, and Regret

Playdates for Mommies — Other People's Kids, Too

Christmas for Mommies — Tinsel, Tantrums, and Too Much Wine

Halloween for Mommies — Costumes, Candy, and Carnage

Summer for Mommies — Sunscreen, Snacks, and Surviving Break

Back to School for Mommies — Finally, Silence (For Five Minutes)

Cooking for Mommies — Dinner: Now With More Complaints!

Cleaning for Mommies — Why Is There Always Glitter?

Budgeting for Mommies — How Many Organ Sales Equal Travel Soccer?

Work-Life Balance for Mommies — Emails in the Bathroom

Technology for Mommies — Screen Time Is a Babysitter

Sleep for Mommies — Just Kidding, You Don't Get That

Marriage for Mommies — Because Someone Has to Find His Keys

Wine for Mommies — It's Not a Problem, It's a Hobby

Coffee for Mommies — Because Sleep Is Dead to You

Printed in Dunstable, United Kingdom